ROUTLEDGE LIBRARY EDITIONS: THE ADOLESCENT

I0127636

Volume 15

THE ADOLESCENT CHILD

THE ADOLESCENT CHILD

W. D. WALL

Routledge
Taylor & Francis Group

LONDON AND NEW YORK

First published in 1948 by Methuen & Co. Ltd

This edition first published in 2023
by Routledge
4 Park Square, Milton Park, Abingdon, Oxon OX14 4RN

and by Routledge
605 Third Avenue, New York, NY 10158

Routledge is an imprint of the Taylor & Francis Group, an informa business

ISBN: 978-1-032-37655-4 (Set)
ISBN: 978-1-032-38711-6 (Volume 15) (hbk)
ISBN: 978-1-032-38715-4 (Volume 15) (pbk)
ISBN: 978-1-003-34641-8 (Volume 15) (ebk)

DOI: 10.4324/9781003346418

Publisher's Note
The publisher has gone to great lengths to ensure the quality of this reprint but points out that some imperfections in the original copies may be apparent.

Disclaimer
The publisher has made every effort to trace copyright holders and would welcome correspondence from those they have been unable to trace.

The
ADOLESCENT CHILD

by

W. D. WALL

Sometime Reader in Education, University of Birmingham

METHUEN & CO. LTD. LONDON
11 New Fetter Lane, E.C.4

First published May 20th 1948
Reprinted seven times
Reprinted 1965

1.8

CATALOGUE NO. 02/3026/46

PRINTED IN GREAT BRITAIN BY BUTLER & TANNER LTD., FROME AND LONDON
AND BOUND BY THE FISHER BOOKBINDING CO. LTD., LONDON

FOREWORD

For a second time a great war has stirred the country into a state of concern about the welfare of youth. Some of those who remember the enthusiasm with which the Fisher Act, after the war of 1914-18, was put forward and the hopes raised by the starting of Continuation schools, are anxious now lest the new Act should fare little better. Still, the prospects seem more hopeful. The raising of the school-leaving age without immediate provision for further part-time education, and with incomplete accommodation and staff, still leaves much to be done; but the increased number of Youth Clubs is a welcome sign.

If, however, the full programme is to be carried out thoroughly and intelligently, we need a still wider knowledge spread among the general public as to the special characteristics of adolescence and its great importance, educationally and vocationally—though some psychologists have been preaching this for wellnigh half a century. Above all it is important that those who deal with adolescents at school, in clubs, or in industry should have as full a knowledge of adolescence as can be gleaned from wide researches as well as from their own experience.

It is for such purposes that this book should be a most valuable help to teachers, club leaders, social and religious workers, and welfare supervisors in factories. The book is packed with good material and based upon a great amount of research, not only in the United States but including much of Dr. Wall's own extensive inquiries. This makes it of special value, as most books on adolescence have dealt entirely, or almost entirely, with American youth. Furthermore, I know that Dr. Wall has proved himself an outstanding success in running a school for young civilian employees in a great military centre. He is himself at home with adolescents of all social levels and the book is fired with enthusiasm for their welfare. This special discussion of the young worker, without secondary education, adds further to the value of this book.

I think that Dr. Wall's views would be substantially accepted by most psychologists in this country. Personally I might want to emphasize, more than he has done, the importance of innate factors in determining the final character of the youth; but it is well for the practical teacher and social worker that the stress should be laid on what is malleable in personality, and that they should not feel themselves hampered in their efforts towards the stimulation of better interests and social development by the material they have to deal with.

It is gratifying to me to reflect that I suggested to Dr. Wall that he should undertake this book and that it is likely to be followed at some time in the future by one of encyclopaedic completeness on the same subject.

C. W. VALENTINE

University of Birmingham   [*Emeritus Professor of*
Education]

ACKNOWLEDGEMENTS

Even so slight a book as this cannot be written without indebtedness to many investigators in many fields. At the risk of appearing pedantic, the writer has cited most of the sources of his information on special points in footnotes, which thus constitute something of a bibliography for those who wish to carry the study of adolescence further than the present book takes it. No writer on the topic can escape a deep and general indebtedness to Stanley Hall, whose *Youth*, and the massive work, *Adolescence*, have been the inspiration of much later research and writing. If specific references to Hall's work are few in the present volume, it is because so much of his material, and the conclusions based upon it, are not directly relevant in our changed social conditions, and it was felt to be better to lean more heavily upon investigations made more recently and upon facts established for groups of English children.

To young people all over the country, and especially to those who joined with me in an educational venture during the last years of the recent war, my debt is great, as it is to those students of mine in the Army and in civil life who so carefully and frankly answered questionnaires and committed their experiences to paper. It is a pleasure too to acknowledge the help of two busy teachers: that of Mr. J. W. Malcolm, who read this book in manuscript and discussed many points of detail with me; and that of Mr. N. Dodman who corrected the page proofs and prepared the index.

My greatest debts, both personal and intellectual, are to Professor Sir Cyril Burt and Professor C. W. Valentine, under both of whom I am proud to say that I have studied. Both have read this book in manuscript and it has gained on almost every page from their generous criticisms and suggestions and from their published researches in the field of psychology. In daily contact with Professor Valentine, first as teacher, and then as friend and colleague, much of this book took shape, and his help and encouragement have been unfailing. Any errors which remain are the responsibility of the author.

W. D. WALL

Birmingham 1947

CONTENTS

			page
	FOREWORD		v
	ACKNOWLEDGEMENTS		vii
	ABBREVIATIONS		x
Chapter I.	WHAT HAPPENS AT ADOLESCENCE?		1
II.	FINDING A SELF		17
III.	LOVE AND FRIENDSHIP		48
IV.	'MOONISH YOUTH'		68
V.	THE MIND GROWS UP		91
VI.	LEARNING TO LIVE		120
VII.	ALL THE WORLD BEFORE THEM		153
VIII.	FULL STATURE		186
	INDEX OF SUBJECTS		201
	INDEX OF NAMES		205

ABBREVIATIONS

B. Journ. P.	*British Journal of Psychology*
B. Journ. Ed. P.	*British Journal of Educational Psychology*
B. Journ. Med. Psych.	*British Journal of Medical Psychology*
F. of Ed.	*Forum of Education*
Gen. Psych. Mon.	*Genetic Psychology Monographs*
I.H.R.B.	*Industrial Health Research Board*
Journ. App. Psych.	*Journal of Applied Psychology*
Journ. Ed. Psych.	*Journal of Educational Psychology* (American)
Journ. Ex. Ped.	*Journal of Experimental Pedagogy*
Journ. Gen. Psych.	*Journal of Genetic Psychology*
Journ. Neur. and Psychopath.	*Journal of Neurology and Psychopathology*
Occ. Psych.	*Occupational Psychology*
Journ. Ment. Sci.	*Journal of Mental Science*

All books are cited for the first time with their place of publication and the date of the edition to which reference is made.

WHAT HAPPENS AT ADOLESCENCE?

Introductory. In the experience of most parents, sometimes with dramatic suddenness, comes a time when they feel that John or Mary is no longer a child. Something indefinable has crept into the expression and behaviour of one who has for years seemed a wholly calculable unit in the family situation. He may become difficult, rebellious. She may be dreamy and unstable, unbiddable and at odds with the world. There may even be sporadic returns to behaviour which had apparently been long ago abandoned, and the thirteen- or fourteen-year-old boy or girl is sometimes surprisingly childish.

Conduct as a whole is often bad in the early teens. Marro,[1] studying Italian boys, found a steady increase in bad behaviour from the age of eleven onwards until it reached its worst at fourteen and then slowly improved. The figures published by many different writers—for example Carr-Saunders[2] and his collaborators—suggest that for boys the peak age for delinquency occurs somewhere between the twelfth and fourteenth years. Girls too appear to be affected, though lassitude and emotional apathy, waywardness, irritability and answering back seem to be more frequent than the more dramatic forms of bad behaviour or real delinquency.

Behaviour difficulties however are only one sign of ferment. In many other directions the personality seems to become again as plastic and variable as it was in nursery years and even to

[1] Cited by Hall, *Youth*, pp. 122–3 (London and New York, 1921).
[2] *Young Offenders*, pp. 52–3 and 121 (Cambridge, 1943).

I

undergo a complete change. Physically, emotionally, and intellectually there seems to be a rapid, though often erratic, development, bewildering at first to parent and teacher (and often to the youth himself) and then, in the later teens, settling to a calmer progress to adulthood.

For some, the transition to the poise and inner harmony which characterize the mature adult is comparatively smooth and easy; for others, it is stormy and vexed: for all, the second decade of life is critical, a time of adjustment to the demands of adult life in the social and economic spheres, and a period when the youth is struggling with emotional impulses which at times threaten to be overwhelming in their strength.

Late Childhood. These developments of the teens often seem the more striking because, for most children, the second half of childhood, which covers the first six or seven years of school life, is a period of relative physical and emotional stability. Both sexes are largely preoccupied with the tangibles of the external world and little given to introspection. Emotionally, this period is the one least liable to upset, for the processes of repression and adaptation, learned but slowly in early days, have reached a satisfactory balance. It is, too, a period of relative indifference to the opposite sex. The boy and girl tend to prefer the companionship of others of their own age and sex. Furfey[1] confirms the findings of earlier investigators who studied the more or less rigidly governed communities which tend to form among children, and describes the 'gang age' as typically a pubescent phenomenon.

Physical Change. This peaceful adequacy to the demands of life does not endure. The most apparent change, at least in the succeeding few years, is physical—the final growth before maturity. Burt[2] has shown that there is little evidence for the

[1] *The Gang Age*, pp. 189 ff. (New York, 1926); see also Moreno, *Who Shall Survive?* (Washington, 1934).
[2] 'The Education of the Young Adolescent', *B. Journ. Ed. P.*, vol. xiii, pt. 3, 1943, p. 128.

view, still held in some medical quarters, that for all children and occurring at roughly the same chronological ages there are periods of rapid growth succeeded by periods of consolidation. Nevertheless, even when we consider average heights and weights for children based upon large numbers measured at each age, there seems to be a perceptible spurt of growth in the teens. For girls, this seems to be earlier by a year, or even two, than for boys, beginning round about eleven and ceasing to be marked after fourteen. The boys seem, on the whole, to start later—at about twelve or thirteen—and finish later at about fifteen.[1] Longitudinal studies based upon repeated measurements of the same children at intervals in their development show that this spurt begins as a rule just before puberty and reaches its maximum in the pubertal year itself. Physical growth, in fact, keeps step, not with chronological but with developmental age.[2]

This would in itself account for some of the increasing variability in growth with which most who have to do with adolescents are familiar. But idiosyncrasies of development tend to be masked by averages. On the whole the tall child tends to become the tall adult and vice versa; but cases are not uncommon where the child of average or below average height may suddenly catch up and even surpass his contemporaries in the teens; and gains of height of six inches or more within a two-year period have been reported.[3] Weight is even less predictable, and there may be periods of over- and under-weight succeeding each other until stability is established in the late teens or early twenties.

Physiological Changes. Increase in weight and height is

[1] See, for example, the tables given in Burt, *The Backward Child*, Appendix 2 (London, 1937), or Simmonds, *Physical Growth and Development*, pp. 16–40 (Monog. of Soc. for Research in Child Development, vol. ix, No. 371 (Washington, 1944).

[2] Simmons, op. cit., pp. 76–81; Dearborn and Rothney, *Predicting the Child's Development*, p. 37 (Cambridge, Mass., 1941); F. D. Brooks, *Child Psychology*, pp. 136–8 (London, 1939).

[3] Arlitt, *Adolescent Psychology*, p. 15 (London, 1937).

accompanied by changes in the internal organs of the body, which directly or indirectly are connected with variations in the glandular balance and, in particular, with the maturation of the sex glands to the point at which the boy or girl becomes sexually fertile. Their total effect is to bring about the full physiological maturity of the individual.

The heart grows larger in proportion to the arteries and veins, and the blood pressure continues to increase. The stomach elongates and becomes more capacious, and, in some cases, there are transitory digestive disorders. The skin undergoes a change which, for a time at least, renders it more than ordinarily sensitive. Neuromuscular control is often temporarily affected—especially in the boy—and even such habitual movements as those involved in handwriting may deteriorate. The speed at which the body uses up energy—the metabolic rate, as it is called—sometimes fluctuates widely, particularly when the psychological balance is disturbed.

In this process of change, temporary disharmonies are very liable to occur, many of which may be traced to anomalies of function in the endocrine or ductless glands, under- or over-function in which may have direct outcome in the emotional life. The thyroid, for example, which is situated in the throat, is sometimes over-active for a time in adolescent girls, producing excitability, febrile energy, tension, and sometimes acute and apparently causeless anxiety. Under-functioning of this gland may result in lethargy and even in a degree of intellectual dulling. The adrenal glands, situated near the kidneys, are intimately involved in fear and anger states and with the development of the secondary sex characteristics. Under- or over-activity of these may accelerate or retard the appearance of the outward signs of maturity, and may, for a time, affect the youth's susceptibility to anger or liability to fatigue.

For most, however, the effect of change is probably much more indirect. Anomalies in functioning may be reflected in precocious physical or physiological changes. These, because they are new and unexpected, or because they appear, in some way, to set the boy or girl apart from contemporaries, tend to become the focus of anxiety. The youth whose voice breaks markedly sooner or later than those of his friends, or the girl who develops, temporarily, symptoms of virilism through an over-activity of the adrenals, is often intensely worried. The writer well remembers an adolescent boy who was acutely distressed by a lopsidedness developing in his forehead—but who dared not mention it to his friends or parents.

Many such variations of growth in the bony structure are due to the functioning of the pituitary gland, found between the roof of the mouth and the base of the brain. Because of its effect on other glands, this has been called 'the conductor of the endocrine orchestra'. Excessive pituitary activity prior to puberty may produce a gigantic stature—even of seven feet or more; under-activity may delay the onset of puberty, lead to arrested physical growth and a great increase of fat. Such marked anomalies are rare, but much slighter ones may cause a degree of physical discomfort or become the centre of tension in social situations. Rapidly enlarging hands and feet, for example, or a nose that seems disproportionately large until the rest of the face catches up, may lead to self-consciousness which is intensified by the well-intentioned, but none the less painful, raillery of friends and adults. 'Gawky' and 'ungainly' are adjectives frequently applied, particularly to the adolescent boy, much to his chagrin and inner torment.

So, too, changes in the digestive system and metabolic rate may sometimes account for food fads, morbid appetites, and the tendency to overeat which are often found among adolescents. It must, however, be remembered that, since it is one of the most purely primitive of tendencies, eating is singularly liable, at any time of life, to become the centre of emotional disturbance. In some cases it has been found that a diet rich in carbohydrates decreases the incidence of morbid appetite and overeating. On the other hand, a marked loss of appetite, even to the point of actual starvation, occurs as a symptom of neurosis in adolescent girls. The converse tendency to overeat, although in part physiologically determined, may also be a manifestation of insecurity and loneliness, a kind of turning back to primitive satisfactions and behaviour in a time of stress.[1]

Puberty. These last examples illustrate the complexity of causation which may underlie emotional developments. They show that in most cases it would be rash to ascribe directly to physiological change what may be either an emotional reaction to the change itself, or the complex product of temperamental, environmental, and physical factors.

This is particularly true of what must be regarded as the central event of adolescence—the attainment of sexual maturity. Physically and emotionally it is of cardinal importance, and it is largely in the light of the onset and attainment of sexual maturity that the phenomena of the teens must be interpreted. Yet we must be on our guard lest we ascribe directly to the physiological action of the sex glands what must rather be looked upon as a product of the total psychological field in which the developing child finds itself. Some time before sexual maturity is properly reached, it is likely that the gonads, stimulated by, and themselves stimulating, the other glands of the endocrine system, are pouring their hormones into the bloodstream, producing premonitory unrest in the organism which penetrates consciousness as a vague uneasiness, almost expectancy. Accompanying it are the physical changes markedly distinguishing the sexes. The girl's form takes on a more rounded contour, the breasts develop, often with considerable pain or irritation. The boy becomes very much aware of his genital apparatus; his voice breaks and is frequently beyond

[1] Blos, *The Adolescent Personality*, pp. 282–3 (New York, 1941). See also Arlitt, op. cit., p. 25; and Henderson and Gillespie, *A Textbook of Psychiatry*, pp. 179 ff. (London, 1944).

control; the beard begins to sprout. In both sexes the growth of axillary and pubic hair is a source of embarrassment at medical examinations and in the dressing-rooms of sports clubs.

In the actual age of onset of puberty there are wide sex and individual differences. With the boy the process is slower and more intermittent than with the girl, to whom menstruation, though perhaps eagerly expected, may come abruptly and as something of a shock. In both sexes there is a wide age range. First menstruation may occur anywhere from 9 to 18 years in girls, although the age range 12 years 8 months to 15 years 8 months will include about two-thirds of a normal English group. The attainment of sexual maturity is on the average later with boys and shows slightly less variation, two-thirds of an English group attaining puberty between 13 years 7 months and 15 years 9 months,[1] though of course individuals will be retarded or advanced outside these limits. Climatic conditions and racial inheritance affect maturity in this respect markedly: inhabitants of temperate and cold climates maturing later than those of Mediterranean and tropical latitudes. Further, those of supernormal intelligence tend to mature earlier and the subnormal to be considerably delayed.[2]

Since the psychological developments of adolescence, in so far as they are produced from within, are closely connected with sexual development, it is not difficult to envisage the problem facing the youth leader or teacher confronted with a group of boys and girls of similar chronological age from about eleven or twelve onwards. Some will be physically and emotionally still children; yet others will be pre-pubescent; yet others will have embarked on adolescence proper; and, at least in the

[1] Burt, The Backward Child, p. 152.
[2] Terman, Genetic Studies of Genius, vol. i, pp. 212 ff. (New York, 1937); Hollingworth, The Psychology of the Adolescent, pp. 22-3 (London, n.d.); Viteles, 'The Influence of Age of Pubescence upon the Physical and Mental Status of Normal School Students', Journ. Ed. Pysch., vol. xx, No. 5.

earlier years, there will be a marked excess of girls relatively more mature than their male contemporaries.

Awareness of Change. With the majority of children these physical changes proceed reasonably smoothly and any anomalies of development are transitory. Nonetheless, awareness of changes, of temporary loss of control, of stronger urges and desires, and the profound redistribution of emotional forces under the impulse of awakening sexual appetites, are bound to have psychological reverberations. Attention is directed on the self: embarrassment, and a lack of social poise, correspond to the physical gaucherie and clumsiness which are proverbial. The boy or girl is reaching out through a new orientation of interests, a new drive towards independence, to the world of adult experience, privilege, and power. The old certainty and adjustment are lost. The new *modus vivendi* is not yet acquired. It is little wonder that some adolescents appear difficult, wayward, and unstable, emotionally as unbalanced as they are physically immature.

It has been the fashion to ascribe most of the intellectual and emotional phenomena of the teens directly to physiological changes, especially to changes in the glandular balance; and thus to regard them as inevitably arising from within. It is difficult to disentangle the effects which slight or great changes in bodily sensations or in physical tone or in output of mental or physical energy may have upon the emotional life of the individual. But it seems fairly certain that it is only in rare cases that a direct physiological cause can be assigned for a particular emotional development, and, even then, the total effect will be dependent upon innate temperamental characteristics, previous life history, and the environmental influences operating at the time. Thus, while physical and physiological growth is, for many children, markedly accelerated during the early teens and especially in the pre-pubertal and pubertal years, the psychology of adolescence must be viewed in the light of the whole mental background of the growing boy or girl, and, in particular, in the light of the conscious and unconscious attitudes adopted by adult society towards the maturing youth.

Primitive Societies. It is characteristic of the *primitive* economy that the transition from child to adult is abrupt. In a savage tribe there is no time for ten years of adolescence, and in particular the adolescent girl seems to be a modern, even a recent, phenomenon.

Primitive societies marked the attainment of puberty with ceremonial; and the initiation of the young into the laws, customs, traditions, and beliefs of the tribe probably represented the earliest attempt at formal education. Severe tests of the capacity to endure pain, to shift for oneself, to withstand the terrors of loneliness, and so on, may have had to be undergone; but the initiation was comparatively brief, and, at the end of a few weeks, the boy or girl was received into full membership of the tribe with the right of grown-up status.[1] Mead[2] writes of the Manu girl of New Guinea that the years following puberty are not, for her, marked by storm and stress: 'they are years of waiting, years which are an uninteresting and not too exacting bridge between the free play of childhood and the obligations of marriage. . . . A girl has no need to seek a husband; he has been found. She may not seek a lover; she is denied the outlet of close friendship with other girls. She simply waits, growing taller and more womanly in figure, and, in spite of herself, wiser in the ways of her world.'

Environmental Provocations. In our society there is no such universal custom officially separating the child from infantile habits and forcing him into adulthood. For many, the abrupt plunge into factory or office after leaving school at fourteen is a

[1] Full accounts of the ceremonials which signalize the advent of puberty among primitive peoples are given by Hall in his *Adolescence* and by Sir J. G. Frazer in *The Golden Bough.* In his book, *The Psycho-Analytic Study of the Family* (London, 1931), pp. 81 ff., Flugel presents the psycho-analytic interpretation of them.
[2] Mead, *Growing up in New Guinea*, p. 111 (Penguin, 1943).

severe initiation, for others, the social and religious observances of 'coming out', presentation at Court, or of confirmation[1] mark a step forward in the attainment of adult status. Increasingly, the complexity and economic advance of our civilization is tending towards a deferment of full entry to the privileges, responsibilities, and rights of the grown-up world. The termination of compulsory education, employment of juveniles, the right to drive a car, to enter a public-house, the age of marriage, of legal responsibility, and the right to vote are all subject to regulation by the law of the country. It is not until the age of twenty-one that a boy or girl can be said to be legally and socially recognized by the community as fully adult, and in many cases, where the need arises for prolonged professional training, the state of tutelage and dependence may continue to the middle twenties or even longer.

Some of the desire to prolong adolescence springs from a recognition of the formative influences at work during the period, and from a wish to protect the growing boy and girl from the consequences of too early an economic pressure. But while it is possible to defer the age of marriage, it is not possible to prevent the attainment of sexual potency; the burden of self-support can be lightened, but the drive towards independence will develop with increasing physical and intellectual maturity. Hence in abandoning the abrupt initiation to the lore of the tribe we have set no perceptible limit to the frustrations with which the developing personality meets in its teens.

Until towards the end of the eighteenth and the beginning of the nineteenth centuries there is, proportionately, very little about the *struggles* of adolescence in literature. Plato's *Dialogues*,

---

[1] In the English and Lutheran Churches this occurs between fourteen and eighteen. The Roman Catholic Communion is earlier. possibly as being originally adjusted to the age of puberty in a Mediterranean climate. The Nonconformist creeds tend to set it later than the Anglican and come more into line with the period of sexual and physical maturity in temperate latitudes and modern communities.

as Hall and Slaughter[1] have pointed out, deal with some of the problems of adolescence though with very little evidence that they are painful crises. The *Confessions* of St. Augustine give a vivid picture of the religious and sexual stresses of a young man. In some of the saga literature, in Saxo Grammaticus, and in our own *Beowulf* are portraits of heroes who, sullen and lazy until the late teens, suddenly rouse themselves to action. Shakespeare too, notably in Hamlet, Romeo, and Troilus, has given subtle studies of young men. In none of these, however, is adolescence treated as a period of special difficulty, or as immune from, or specially subject to, developmental stresses. Rousseau's *Émile* and his later *Confessions*, Blake's *Book of Thel* and *Songs of Experience* do however begin to treat adolescence as a psychological and pedagogical problem. With the rise of the Romantic movement in England, the singers of the *mal de siècle* in France, and the followers of Wertherism in Germany and elsewhere, we find the psychic disturbances, and above all, the sadness and depression of the adolescent, capitalized as one of the most poignant themes of literature. *Le Lac, Epipsychidion*, and *Wilhelm Meister*, each in its characteristic way, deal with some of the many aspects of adolescent emotions and preoccupations. It is not without significance that this marked increase in the treatment of adolescence as a literary theme should coincide with the beginning of the industrial revolution. It lends colour to the view put forward by Trotter,[2] Hollingworth, and others, that in our culture there are, for the adolescent, provocations to upset not so strongly presented to the child or to the adult. Ruth Benedict, too, points out that although it is a fact of nature that a child becomes a man or woman 'the way in which this transition is effected varies from one society to another and no one of these particular cultural bridges should be regarded

[1]Hall, *Adolescence*, vol. 1, ch. viii (New York, 1916); Slaughter, *The Adolescent*, p. 5 (London, 1919).
[2] Trotter, *The Instincts of the Herd in Peace and War*, pp. 49–50 (London, 1916); Hollingworth, op. cit., pp. 222–3.

as the "natural" path to maturity.'[1] Further, as two distinguished investigators[2] of the field agree, the average adult reacts as if the problems raised by the clash of the developing boy or girl with the environment are in fact the problems of adolescence itself.

An interesting confirmation of the view that at least the age of incidence of many adolescent dilemmas is determined by the environment is given by Burt,[3] who compiled a list of the mental, moral, and emotional characteristics generally attributed to adolescents, and asked a number of teachers at what age, in their opinion, the changes mentioned seemed most noticeable. The replies showed that teachers in elementary schools gave at or soon after fourteen; in grammar schools, about seventeen or eighteen; in university departments, about nineteen to twenty-one, while in postgraduate institutions it was often put as late as twenty-two or twenty-three. Such evidence cannot of course be pressed too far, but it does seem to indicate that many of the mental phenomena of adolescence which we shall be discussing in detail in succeeding chapters are precipitated by social factors and especially by the age at which the child is called on to face the responsibilities of the adult worker.[4]

Nor should it be forgotten that in recent writing, more especially in the literary treatment of adolescence, the emphasis has been upon the youth of supernormal intelligence. Terman[5] in his study of one thousand gifted children concludes that a really high level of intelligence tends to make its possessor have

[1] Benedict, 'Continuities and Discontinuities in Cultural Conditioning', *Psychology*, vol. i, May 1938.
[2] Cole, *The Psychology of Adolescence*, pp. 9–10 (London, 1936). Partridge *The Social Psychology of Adolescence*, pp. 12–13 (Prentice Hall, 1939).
[3] Burt, art. cit., p. 128.
[4] An interesting case study is cited in *Biographies of Child Development* (Gesell et al.). It concerns a girl who menstruated at the age of three and a half. In spite of this physical precocity, however, she showed the characteristic mental and emotional developments of adolescence in the teens and not, as might have been expected, with a comparable degree of prematurity.
[5] op. cit., vol. iii, pp. 183 and 265.

considerably more difficulty in making social adjustments; and that while adult genius is mobile and can seek out its own kind, the highly intelligent child, who may be mentally advanced by as much as five or more years at adolescence, can choose companions only from its contemporaries. Further, physical and social maturity, though perhaps in advance of chronological age, is likely in such cases to lag behind the intellectual.

Much therefore of the picture of storm and stress and of unhappiness which marks the literary presentation of adolescence must be ascribed to the maladjustments and difficulties with which the supernormal and abnormal adolescent meets in adapting to an environment largely peopled by those of lesser intellectual maturity than himself. Much of it too is incident to our culture pattern, which concedes social and economic maturity only by degrees, imposing restraints without at the same time offering adequate sublimations.[1]

The Chaos of Values. Perhaps even more important than this is the fact that our society offers to the young no coherent pattern of universally accepted values. To the adolescent in most primitive cultures the tribe offered a single code of sex morals, few and simple vocational choices, comparatively rigid and uncomplicated rules of social behaviour, and a religion which permitted only degrees of belief and unbelief. Very different is the picture in Britain or any developed western civilization.[2] The adolescent is surrounded by uncertainty and conflict in almost every department of life. In matters of sex, monogamy is sanctioned by law and custom, and premarital chastity is the accepted code; but advocates of great prestige

---

[1] It is interesting to note that where adults (as in static units of the Army) are placed in an environment which deprives them of a measure of independence, puts restraint upon sexual activity, and offers frustrations and thwartings similar to those which modern conditions impose upon the developing boy and girl, the result is a marked increase in moodiness, in horseplay, in increased alcoholism and seeking for excitement, and in sex behaviour which is markedly 'adolescent' in its expression.

[2] This matter is dealt with very fully in relation to the conditions of American society by Margaret Mead, in *Coming of Age in Samoa* (New York, 1936).

will be found forwarding the claims of sexual experiment, companionate marriage, total celibacy, premarital licence, one moral standard for both sexes, differential standards of sex morals for men and women, and so on. The nearest relatives may be prudish in outlook, while a beloved and admired uncle is free and uninhibited. Vocational choice appears unlimited and the multiplicity of possible careers is exceeded only by the difficulty of obtaining information about them. As contacts with adult society widen, differences in manners and conventions seem more marked. In one group a local accent is condemned—in another accepted. At the house of one friend, courteous behaviour is gently insisted upon—at another's laughed at. Wide differences in family discipline are revealed. In one family Jack has a door-key and is allowed to come in at eleven o'clock, in another William is obliged to be in by eight and account for all his movements. Jill is given ample pocket-money, uses cosmetics, chooses her own clothes, calls her parents by their Christian names. Shelagh is accompanied almost everywhere by her mother, wears clothes that are labelled 'sensible' rather than attractive, and is taught to regard lipstick as fast and men as potentially dangerous animals. In religious matters the choice is bewildering. The family group may show as many shades of belief or unbelief as there are members; outside, dozens of sects are clamant that theirs is the right and the only way. Politics, ideals, tastes, interests, ambitions, manners, morals—all these and a hundred other most important departments of mental and emotional life offer tangled avenues among which, with more or less conflict, a choice must be made, and that at a time when, even on the physical plane, inner harmony has not been achieved.

A Happy Time. When all this is allowed for, the period from eleven or twelve to eighteen or twenty is seen as one of crucial importance in the formation of the adult personality. But it is not to be thought of as a time, necessarily, of abrupt and startling change, in which entirely *new* emotions and faculties mysteriously arise from within, but as continuous with, and growing out of, childhood. Physical growth, impending maturity, and an intensification in the emotional life combine to make it a time when environmental friction is peculiarly liable to develop, especially in our complex and incoherent society; but in spite of this, it can be a steady, more or less undisturbed process of adjustment to the new power of sex on the one hand, and to the demands of the adult world on the other.

Such, in fact, for many it seems to be. Symonds[1] found that 52 per cent. of a group of high school pupils, 30 per cent. of college, and 34 per cent. of graduate students agreed that life was going smoothly and peacefully, or that they were full of deep joy; whereas of all groups, less than 3 per cent. described themselves as 'restless, impatient, uncertain, dull, cross, confined, anxious, irritated, gloomy, miserable . . . no pleasure in anything'. Of the youngest group 46 per cent., 67 per cent. of the college group, and 68 per cent. of the graduate school group indicated that they were 'contented at times and at other times discontented; life has both favourable and unfavourable aspects'. Evidence collected by the present writer from young men and women of all levels of intelligence supports a similar conclusion. Out of 79 men 63 (80 per cent.) stated that they found the years from thirteen to twenty-one predominantly happy; 4 were doubtful, and, of the 12 who stated that they were unhappy during the period, only 3 stated that their childhood had been happy, the remaining 9 found childhood also a period of unhappiness. In a group of 136 women, the picture is the same. 118 (87 per cent.) of them stated that their adolescence was happy: of the 15 who did not, 4 were also unhappy in their childhood and 1 lost father and brother as she was growing to maturity.

[1] 'Happiness as related to Problems and Interests', *Journ. Ed. Psych.*, vol. xxviii, No. 4, 1937.

This does not rule out the thesis that, for some, the process of adjustment and of building an adult self is difficult and painful; or that for many, adolescence is liable to *temporary* emotional upset and instability. It does however suggest that storm and stress, violent mood fluctuations, depression and the rest, are not universal and inevitable concomitants of growth: they are rather to be looked at as manifestations of difficulty in adjustment, of insecurity or frustration. This is a hopeful conclusion for those who have adolescent children or who work among growing boys and girls: for it appears likely that by careful study of individual adolescents, and of the general psychological trends of the period, and by skilful adjustment of the environment, much can be done to help the young reach maturity with the minimum of conflict and disturbance.

Certain features, both biological and social, must be accepted as unalterable. Physical growth and sexual development can be neither delayed nor accelerated. Between childhood and maturity, the boy or girl in our civilization has to become a social personality in his own right and wean him or herself from dependence on father or mother; he or she has to make an adjustment in the sexual life and come to terms with one of the most powerful of the instinctive drives. Most have also to find an economic self, seeking through work the foundation of independence and of marriage. In their several ways and on very different levels, each boy and girl, too, has to work out some interpretive philosophy. These are formidable tasks. A knowledge of them, of the laws of growth, and of the strains to which the growing personality is adapting, will enable parent and teacher to help each of their charges to achieve a balanced and integrated personality which is the foundation of happiness and success.

CHAPTER II

FINDING A SELF

I. THE CHANGING ENVIRONMENT

Awareness of Difference. Some of the psychological change apparent in the teens must be attributed to a growing awareness of difference, of the ways in which 'I' am different from 'them'. Reference has already been made to the wide age range within which sexual maturity is attained. Differences arising from this cause are accentuated by the lack of close correlation between intellectual maturity, physical growth, and emotional development. Environmental variations emphasize the biological divergence; and idiosyncrasies of development, of acquired attitudes, and so on, tend to maximize and draw attention to the lack of uniformity in the group in which the boy or girl finds himself or herself.

Before the age of twelve, most children are at school; it is safe to predict that the majority of a group of boys will like adventure stories, prefer the society of their own sex, and be little inclined to introspection. Three or four years later, some will have been at work for a year or more, others will be sitting for important examinations and looking forward to years of professional training, yet others will be thinking of leaving school and wondering about a job. One boy will be avidly reading 'bloods', be markedly extrovertive, and still inclined mainly for the society of his own sex; another may have turned away almost entirely from reading, be wildly enthusiastic about sport, and have marked heterosexual interests; whilst a third

3

may have embarked upon the task of acquiring encyclopaedic knowledge like Benjamin Franklin and be passing through a phase of withdrawal and introspection. Among girls, particularly in the *early* teens, the range of variation may be wider. In fact a miscellaneous group of young people between say twelve and fifteen will exhibit greater heterogeneity in every way than it has shown before—perhaps than it will ever show again when once the greater rigidity of the adult world has imposed its more limited patterns.

Environmental Frictions. This awareness of development and consciousness of difference may be fostered by a far-reaching change in the relative importance of the home environment for many in the teens. The nature and direction of this change and some of its effects on mental life are shown by a study made by the author of 73 young women, all between the ages of eighteen and twenty-one and all in the two-year teacher training department of a university. The number of subjects involved is small and they are a highly selected sample of above average ability; and it is within these limitations that the results must be interpreted. Each was asked to jot down in absolute confidence those things in her childhood and adolescent experience which had caused her happiness or unhappiness. The results throw a clear light on the way in which the emotional atmosphere in which the adolescent lives differs from that of the child.

Even when we allow for the greater recency of adolescent experience and the way in which painful memories tend to fade, the study suggests an increase of environmental friction in the teens. Over three-quarters of the group rated themselves as being on the whole happy at both periods of their lives; but of the 214 factors mentioned as stimuli to happiness or unhappiness in adolescence, nearly half are stated to have caused unhappiness, whereas of the 195 factors remembered from childhood, only a quarter are mentioned as having been productive of unhappiness.

More striking is the evidence provided of the change in relative importance of environmental stimuli. Nearly all the group mention circumstances of *home life* in childhood as being productive of happiness or unhappiness (two-thirds as a source of happiness and rather less than a third as a source of unhappiness). Only just over half the group mention home circumstances as stimuli in adolescence—rather less than a quarter stating that factors in the home brought happiness, while one-third mention painful clashes with parents, brothers or sisters.

This decline in the importance of the home in adolescence is matched by an increase in mentions of *school and university*. Well under half the group mention happenings at school as a source of emotional stimulus in childhood (one-third as a source of happiness and one-tenth as a source of unhappiness): but the events and personalities of school and university are mentioned by three-quarters of the group as of importance to them in their teens (by between one-third and one-half as a source of happiness, and by one-third as a source of unhappiness). A similar trend is shown in the mentions made of various *social activities*. These are mentioned by fewer than one-fifth as a source of happiness or unhappiness in childhood but by nearly a third of the group in adolescence.

In three other fields there are changes worthy of note. Such more or less *abstract* things as religion, nature, injustice, and growing-up are mentioned only by two students as having been of importance in their childhood, but a fifth of the group mention them in adolescence, predominantly as sources of unhappiness. The converse is true of such more or less *objective* things as treats, money, presents, which are mentioned by few as of importance in adolescence but by a fifth of the group as sources, mainly of happiness, in childhood. The beauty or otherwise of the *physical environment*, life in the country or by the seaside, the distresses or comforts of evacuation and so on are commented on by a quarter of the group as of importance in adolescence and by fewer than 8 per cent. in childhood.

The experiences reported by this group indicate that even those whose lives are comparatively sheltered enter a wider world in their teens. Youths with different vocational aims and of different levels of ability or economic or social circumstances may meet with more dramatic transformations in the transition from school to working life. For others, awakening may come by joining a Youth Club, leaving home, or entering the sixth form of a grammar school. For the majority, there seems to be a tendency, more or less marked, for groups outside the home and immediate family circle to exert more influence in the mental life. In part, the change may be due to the break in the daily continuity of existence which comes with school-leaving. Something too may perhaps be ascribed to the desire to be grown-up, to an increasing gregariousness, and to rising heterosexual interests. The indirectly expressed attitudes of adult society, the ideas which are held by many grown-ups of what should be expected of boys and girls of a given age, also play their part.

This widening of the social sphere is an aspect of the process of emancipation from the narrower and more intense influence of the home and the parents. It is only to be expected that it will be productive, at least temporarily, of heightened emotional tension. Even a well-balanced and confident man or woman feels some sense of insecurity when plunged into a society whose code and conventions are unfamiliar. The growing boy or girl has, as a rule, no reserve of self-confidence born of success, no habitual defences, on which to call. Until these are acquired there will be an emotional *qui vive* to all kinds of stimuli and possibly a rapid and extensive modification of emotional attitudes.

Consciousness of the Physical Self. Stresses arising from this general change in the social field tend to make more vivid the experience of the self. They may profoundly change or modify attitudes towards others in the environment and, in particular, they are likely to affect the conception of the self in relation to others, contemporaries and adults.

In the early teens and with children of average intelligence the growing preoccupation with the self may strike no deeper than a concern largely with externals. We may perhaps best illustrate the extent and nature of this from an investigation (reported in more detail in Chapters IV and V) with 196 adolescent boys and girls, most of whom were under sixteen and all of whom came from working or lower-middle class homes. Two-thirds of the boys and over four-fifths of the girls report that their interest in their own personal appearance has increased since the age of thirteen. Over half the girls and nearly half the boys state that, since thirteen, they have taken an increased interest *in the impression which they make on others* by their personal appearance, by the things they can do, by the way in which they speak, and by their manners and behaviour. Parallel to this are the proportions of the group (nearly two-thirds of the boys and over three-quarters of the girls) who also state that their interest in dancing, clubs, parties, societies, gangs, and all forms of social activity, has intensified.

Sex Difference in Social Interests. With the girl, the increased interest in social activities and in her own personality as it strikes others is matched by an equal preoccupation with social relationships in general. This is not so strikingly found in boys of the same age though it may develop later. The group mentioned above was asked to write down in confidence the questions to which they would most like to know the answers. Of the questions asked by the girls, a quarter are directly concerned with problems of sex behaviour: 'the right age to marry' —'when should boys be taken seriously'—'Is it natural to be shy with boys?'—and so on; a further 16 per cent. concern the attitudes of parents and other adults towards going out with boys, going to the cinema and to dances, the use of cosmetics and the like; and rather less than 10 per cent. are concerned with more or less general social attitudes: 'Why are German and Italian prisoners despised?'—'Why do people resent American soldiers?' Of all the questions asked by girls, just over two-thirds are concerned with problems of direct personal and social reference, and less than a quarter with current affairs or matters of objective fact.

The picture presented by the boys is different. Of their questions, nearly one-third concern current affairs—the outcome of the war, the fate of Hitler, conditions after the war, politics, and so on; a further quarter ask for enlightenment about matters of scientific fact—the size of the sun, the possibility of perpetual motion, the speed at which the earth is cooling, the precise way in which an aeroplane keeps in the air, the possibilities of a cure for tuberculosis. In all, rather more than half the boys' questions are thus objective; and rather less than a quarter are concerned with personal social problems.

A very similar trend to that noted above is shown in a far wider research into the curiosity of children carried out by W. A. Simson.[1] He found that sex, human relationships, and the self were, respectively, third, fourth, and fifth in the list of interests of thirteen-year-old girls from all types of school but that they ranked fifth, seventh, and ninth for boys of the same age. In older, grammar-school groups, sex remained the principal field of curiosity with the girls, rising to a peak at the age of sixteen, whereas in the lists of contemporary boys it achieved nothing higher than third place. Throughout the same period human relationships are of greater interest to the girls, and at the age of seventeen are third in importance on their lists, whereas with the boys this topic never rises higher than fifth place.

Some of the difference, shown in these two researches, between the interests of boys and girls may represent an enduring core of sex difference—men having more practical and fewer social interests than women. Some of it too can be ascribed to

[1] *An Inquiry into Curiosity as shown in the Written Questions of Children and Adolescents* (November, 1946). Thesis for the Degree of M.A. in the Library of the University of Birmingham.

the generally earlier sexual maturity of the girl and to the more dramatic form which the onset of puberty takes for her. This would tend to direct her attention to matters of sex and to social attitudes to heterosexual adjustment. Much however is to be traced directly to the different social pressures experienced by the sexes, to the different standards of behaviour expected from girls in lower-middle-class and working-class homes, and to the atmosphere of interest in boys which is prevalent in such groups, but which is often quite absent in groups of a similar age in more sheltered conditions.

Special Points of Strain. Around these developing attitudes and at almost any point, stresses may develop, and especially in the sphere of sex. We shall discuss sex developments in some detail in the next chapter: here it may be pointed out that the desires arising from sexual potency itself and the fears which, through wrong training and misinformation, tend to gather round the earlier manifestations, may provoke more or less serious inner disturbances which sometimes issue indirectly in conflict with the environment. Most primitive communities have sought to curb the direct expression of the sex drive; and in modern Britain it is hedged around with prohibition, silence, taboos, and rigid convention. The ideas of indecency and dirtiness, of social or religious prohibition which surround the idea of sex in its physical aspects are often, in the mind of the growing youth, inextricably entangled with an increased interest in the opposite sex—the early tentative flirtations, sensations of shyness, and so on. Sexual activity too, in the eyes of many boys and girls, is one—and not the least impressive—of the symbols of adulthood; and the possession of a boy or girl friend is essential to self-respect. Cinemas, glossy magazines, advertisements, novelettes, all exploit, often in its crudest form, this powerful drive and excite the appetites of the young. It is small wonder that for some, even for many for a time, anxieties, feelings of guilt, and inexplicable uneasiness develop. The writer well remembers an adolescent boy who secretly treasured for more than a twelvemonth a corset advertisement. He was compulsively drawn to scrutinize it minutely from time to time but always with a feeling of guilt. And yet he was unable to part with it until, with a sudden revulsion of shame, he tore it in pieces after reading a book which recommended purity in thought, word, and deed. This must be but one of many similar cases whose development shows no later abnormality. Where no adequate and socially approved outlets for the sex drive are available in the eight or ten years which intervene between the attainment of sexual maturity and the age at which marriage becomes possible, the pent-up forces of the sex life must find some outlet—the danger is that it may be explosive or otherwise undesirable.

Closely bound up with this are the attitudes, conscious and unconscious, adopted by adults to the manifestations of maturity in the young. Flügel[1] suggests that in many puberty ceremonials there is implicit an element of hostility to the younger generation and that some such unconscious motivation underlay the examinations of the mediaeval universities. The attainment of full physical vigour is a challenge to the prestige and power of the generation in control. Growth in intelligence, and the widening field of interests which comes with emotional change, may lead the youth to throw down an intellectual gauntlet in politics, religion, or the minute details of home life. Fathers, schoolmasters, and the grown-up world generally, too often rebut such callow challenges by repressive or derisory measures, reacting with ill-disguised fear against the threat to their long unchallenged dominance. It is not uncommon for the spinster schoolmistress or supervisor of young girls to rationalize her jealousy of their budding attractiveness by accusing them of frivolity: or to compensate for an unconscious hostility by an excessive zeal for their welfare. Deeply repressed sex fears and

[1] *Man, Morals and Society*, pp. 128 ff. (London, 1945).

inhibitions in parents sometimes lead to cramping restrictions being laid upon the developing interests and friendships of the child. Few adults seem able to preserve an attitude of tolerant, uninvolved friendliness which concedes, as to an equal, the right to independence.

Rebellion. The development of such stresses in the early teens is shown by the replies of the group of young adolescents mentioned earlier, to a question asking them to state the things over which they felt inclined to rebel. Among the girls, conflicts over the discipline of the home are frequently mentioned —especially where this seems to involve injustice or different standards applied to various members of the family. One writes that she feels rebellious 'when I am not allowed to go out like other girls and when I have to do most of the work at home and my sisters don't do any'; another, 'The time I'm allowed to stop out at night, make-up, and clothes'; and another, 'When I want to wear my best clothes for work and my mother won't let me'. Very frequently occurs, 'Not being able to go to the pictures as often as I like'. This kind of cause of friction is not mentioned by the boys, among whom the difficulties seem to occur rather outside the home. 'Being not able to have free speech without getting into trouble', says one. 'Things which I believe in and cannot do or say; also having to take orders off people who are not in the position, either mentally or physically, to do so,' writes another. Common to both sexes, and marked in both, is a rebellious reaction to injustice, sarcasm, and lack of understanding. 'Over sarcasm and not understanding', replies one girl; 'favouritism', 'unfairness', 'her sarcastic remarks', 'being snapped at for something which could be explained without', 'Not being able to tell my part of the story', 'Things which they have said to you', write others; and the boys— 'Stubbornness of non-comprehending people', 'Because you do your best and you get shouted at', 'Undeserved punishment', 'Bosses' favourites bossing you about', 'Not being able to speak my mind without raising ill-feelings against myself'.

Two interesting American researches confirm and illuminate the findings from this group. Among 8,000 adolescents, Burgess[1] found that only the girls mentioned their dress and the right to go to unchaperoned parties as sources of friction with their parents; whereas direct criticism, especially of their fathers, was characteristic of boys. In another research, reported by Cole,[2] into the causes of anger, and fear in childhood, adolescence, and maturity, puts it into a wider context. In childhood, it seems, 75 per cent. of the stimuli causing anger are provided by someone trying to take away a plaything or by conflicts over dressing and toilet: and fear seems to be caused by violence of all kinds from persons, natural phenomena, accidents, and so on. Adults still show irritability with material objects but more commonly are annoyed when work or leisure are interfered with, and there is some concern over abstract justice or *impersonal* social situations. Among adolescents, especially girls, social situations, and in particular personal slights are the predominant incitements to anger; and, while the adult fears a threat to his job or health, the youth is afraid primarily of situations in which he or she will appear at a disadvantage, as well as of actual disease and accidental violence.[3]

Self-analysis. Such experiences as we have been discussing, of frustration, antagonism, or ridicule from adults or contemporaries—and who escapes some at least?—turn the attention inwards; and by them, self-awareness may be deepened to minute introspective analysis. Consciousness of individuality is no new development in adolescence; it may, in fact, as Allport[4]

---

[1] Cited by Partridge, *The Social Psychology of Adolescence*, pp. 197-8, 205-7.
[2] op. cit., pp. 63-4.
[3] This should be compared with the closely similar findings based on the author's group and reported in detail in Chapter IV.
[4] *Personality: A Psychological Interpretation*, pp. 161-5 (London, 1938). Compare also the evidence given by Valentine, *The Difficult Child and the Problem of Discipline*, pp. 6-7 (London, 1940), that a period of revolt and self-assertion is normal between the ages of two and four.

points out, be traced to early childhood, to the age at which the personal pronouns are used correctly at about two and a half. But even at five or more the child continues to confuse himself in play with the figures he is impersonating and to identify his private fantasies with objective fact. What is different rather is the increasing hold upon the distinction between 'I' and the rest of mankind, and the increasing complexity of the sentiment of the self which grows up in the teens. It is one aspect of the transition from the more or less egocentric, simple, and comparatively unself-conscious personality of the child adapted to a few social relationships to the more subtle self-awareness of the adult adapted to a complex series of social relationships.

This may proceed by a series of gradual modifications, or apparently by a single dramatic happening, trivial in itself, but explosively apt for development. Meredith, in *The Ordeal of Richard Feverel*, describes how the threat of a medical examination and the wounded pride at being whipped accelerated the mental and emotional growth of his hero in one afternoon. For others, small happenings, chance remarks of companions, unimportant in other contexts and at other ages, assume immense importance and are remembered long afterwards as marking a turning-point and as provoking moments of intense self-scrutiny and self-knowledge.

Introspectiveness, consciousness of individuality, and uncertainties of adjustment make even such familiar situations as the home full of emotional stimuli. Patterns of behaviour acceptable in the child are being abandoned but adequate adult techniques have not been acquired; hence many boys and girls are unsure of themselves and of their behaviour in the more or less novel situations in which they find themselves as the result of growth and of coming into contact with the social world. For some, a closely knit family group provides the necessary support; for others a 'crowd', or club, or a form at school, or a society, gives the acceptance that is craved; others—especially girls—form devoted friendships which supply the apparently necessary prop; yet others do not seem—so even is their development—to need a framework within which to find security. Very many, for a time at least, seem to be in danger of losing their identity and imitate slavishly the conventions, slang, dress, and interests of the club, friend, or group of the moment. Others surreptitiously compare themselves with companions and consciously try to improve this or that in their appearance, manners, or behaviour, or else they con avidly books of etiquette or write for advice to popular magazines. Some seem morbidly sensitive to slights real or imaginary, to public opinion—especially in the years up to seventeen—and show a marked lack of humour where anything concerning the self—dress, manners, behaviour, and so on—is concerned. One or two are unstable and perplexed to a marked degree and others withdrawn and morose for a time.

All these and the many other shades of adolescent behaviour are signs of stress, of uncertainties of adjustment, and anxieties of all kinds. Their development under the impact of environmental and physiological change does something to account for the moods of intense dejection reported by two-thirds of Valentine's men students and by three-quarters of his group of women students, and for the thoughts of suicide reported by over a third of the men and over a quarter of the women.[1]

Valentine's is a rather special sample 'of high general intelligence, and the problems of adjustment for a younger and more nearly average group may not be so severe: but it would be a mistake to underestimate (as many adults are prone to do) the intensity of the distresses experienced by some boys and girls. Equally erroneous would it be (as was stressed in Chapter I) not to recognize that adolescence is, for many if not for most,

[1] Valentine, 'Adolescence and Some Problems of Youth Training', *B. Journ. Ed. P.*, vol. xiii, pt. 2, p. 58.

also a period of quickened responsiveness to pleasureable stimuli, a surge of the pure joy of living. In this, as in most things, the range of variation is probably very great. So too there is great variation in the nature of the environmental factors which are brought to bear, even on individuals in the same social group. The boy or girl in the teens is so subject to change in the psychological atmosphere and there is so great a likelihood that internal and external stresses will coincide, that few children in our culture escape some quickening of the emotional tempo. It is this quickened responsiveness which mades the second decade of life crucial for the development of personality.

II. MEETING THE ENVIRONMENT

In the means by which the growing boy or girl copes with these problems of mental growth and forms an adult personality, we may make a rough division. We can distinguish between those reactions which involve an attempt to evade or withdraw from the demands which are made on adaptability and those which carry the personality forward to a closer harmony with things as they are. This distinction, as will be seen later, is in some degree artificial. Nor should it be supposed that one process is at any time likely to be in sole possession of the psychological field. Human behaviour is complex, its determinants subtle and often indirect. concealed from the person himself as much or more than from the observer. At one and the same time the adolescent boy or girl may be vigorously adapting in one sphere of mental life and be in retreat in another. Similar forms of behaviour too may arise from very different underlying causes. We can, however, with these provisos, study some of the processes involved and some of the ways in which they show themselves in behaviour.

In very many, in the early teens at all events, protective reactions seem most marked—possibly because in children of average and below average intelligence the fourteenth has been the school-leaving year and the fifteenth the year of adjustment to the demands of a job. For the boy or girl in the grammar school too the fifteenth year, which brings the challenge of an important external examination or the beginning of preparation for it, is often a markedly difficult one.[1] The first half of the teens too is the time during which the majority of children attain puberty, an event which presents not a few with painful emotional problems. We may profitably begin then with a discussion of some of the processes by which the mind strives to defend itself against emotional pressures.

Negativism. Where the boy and girl feel themselves threatened by overwhelming emotion, there may be an attempt to reject the situation entirely, a refusal to do anything, a marked and intense contra-suggestibility directed against any person or circumstance in the environment which attempts to push the personality forward to cope with the problem. Such a phase of *negativism*, as it is called, is characteristic of the behaviour of the two-year-old just at the time when a sense of personal integrity is growing.[2] A repetition of an even more pervasive kind has been noted in boys and girls just prior to puberty. It may take a generalized form like that shown by a fourteen-year-old girl of the writer's acquaintance, whose 'I don't *want* to' was so automatic a response to any suggestion that it became a matter for jokes between herself and the adults with whom she worked. It may show itself as a persistent argumentativeness, answering back, and even impudence, so irritating to parents whose authority has never hitherto been questioned. Or it may appear as a disinclination to make any exertion, physical or mental, for long periods together.[3]

[1] See Chapter VI.
[2] See page 26 and footnote 4.
[3] Hollingworth, *Handbook of Child Psychology*, ed. Murchison, p. 900 (Massachusetts, 1933), following Hildegard Hetzer. See also the contribution to the same book by Charlotte Bühler, p. 389; Bühler, *From Birth to Maturity*, p. 196 (London, 1937); and Deutsch, *The Psychology of Women*, vol. i, pp. 5–11 (New York, 1944).

Retreat. Closely allied to this defensive contra-suggestibility are what may be called the mechanisms of retreat. When life becomes too difficult, the growing boy or girl may go back, *regress*, as the psychologist calls it, to childish behaviour—temper tantrums or other ways of protest—which have brought relief in the past. All of us are familiar with adolescents unusually childish at times in their behaviour, and if this reaction becomes fixed and carried over into adult life we get the picture of the adult 'Peter Pan'.

Regressive behaviour may show itself in a great variety of forms, not all of which can be dealt with here. The boy or girl may show fear of impending change by anxiously clinging to parents and suffering acute home-sickness if they have to be left even for a short time. Others show their anxiety or repressed aggressiveness by a return to bed-wetting—though this usually suggests a very deep-seated maladjustment in the emotional life. Some make the attempt to discard all responsibilities and are as unreliable as a young child. In some, egocentricity and the crude desire to attract attention at all costs express themselves in childish or markedly antisocial forms.

Day-dreaming. The desire to retreat from the difficult demands of life may result in an attempt to enjoy in imagination what hard reality denies. A glance at the figures of Table 2, Chapter IV, will show that a large proportion of adolescents report an increase in day-dreaming since the age of thirteen. Such compensatory fantasies offer a refuge within which the world may be refashioned to the heart's desire without the need to adjust to the demands of hard reality. Varendonck[1] has shown how such more or less undirected thinking proceeds either at or just below the level of consciousness in all of us and stems from deep unconscious causes, urges, and desires, such as also find expression in nocturnal dreams. Fantasy too is an important element in creative activity and ambition; it is a kind

[1] *The Psychology of Day Dreams* (New York, 1921).

of mental play in which modes of behaviour and sources of satisfaction can be experimentally tried out. For most adolescents, as for most adults, it provides merely a temporary refuge from the inevitable frustrations of life, and the hold on reality is never more than briefly abandoned. Fantasy becomes dangerous when the fine edge between imagination and reality is lost, when the personality is too weak and the external pressures are too strong and the boy or girl comes to accept fantasies as realities. Implicit in thinking is the tendency to action, and the day-dream world may seek issue in bragging or lying, for example. The latter is particularly characteristic of the maladjusted adolescent girl in whom it may come to the pitch where she firmly believes her own fantasies and is half-way to serious psychopathic delusion.[1] The adolescent boy who is suffering from feelings of inadequacy or thwarted self-assertion may seek to give substance to his dreams by thefts, the proceeds of which are used to buy popularity among his fellows. Sometimes sex fantasies become compulsive and issue in obscene scribblings or, as in the case of one boy of the author's acquaintance, in obscene remarks made over the telephone from the anonymity of a public kiosk.

More serious in its consequences may be the complete withdrawal from all contact with the real world. In such cases the boy or girl seems more and more to be refusing the task of adaptation, becoming more and more morose and shut in, until at last ruminations seem to absorb all the emotional energy. The patient becomes sunk in lethargy, indifferent to all environmental stimuli; there is little appreciation of what is going on around, and there may be delusions and hallucinations. The condition may start with a more than usually marked increase in the time spent in reading coupled with a noticeable decline in the quality of school work, and proceed until we have the picture of fully developed schizophrenia, as it is called. Such

[1] Burt, *Young Delinquent*, pp. 384 ff. (London, 1938); Hart, *Psychopathology*, pp. 107-8 (Cambridge, 1927); H. D. Williams, 'Causes of Social Maladjustment in Young Children, *Univ. of Iowa Studies in Psych.*, No. xv, 1932, p. 208

developments are comparatively rare though this form of mental disease increases in frequency in the second decade of life, rising to a peak at about twenty-five. In most cases (50–60 per cent.) there is a family history of mental illness and even more usually there are peculiarities of development in childhood and young adolescence.[1] From our point of view, the important thing is that a few boys and girls—especially those of a shy, sensitive type—may develop similar reactions in the teens which if not met and dealt with may become habitual failures of adaptation. *Markedly* excessive reading which seems to have little object except the gratification of fantasy, self-absorption, marked and prolonged withdrawal from social contacts and activities, lasting depression, are signs that normal adjustments to life are not being made.

Projection. Other mechanisms directed at the protection of the immature self from the pressure of circumstances have been distinguished by psychologists. In some boys and girls, secret wishes, fears, or feelings of inferiority are powerful and at the same time repression prevents them from being fully recognized for what they truly are. Such youths are liable to *project* onto persons or things in the environment, the very thoughts of their own minds. Adolescents who blame their 'luck' for a misfortune which springs from an obvious lack of effort, or who believe themselves the object of an unjust persecution, are examples. Perhaps some of the fears expressed by adolescent girls of dark places at night, of rough men and foreigners, are projections, in a tangible form, of repressed sex wishes; and the boys who fear torture at the hands of the Japanese, or 'interplanetary catastrophes', may be projecting onto the environment their own destructive, aggressive impulses.[2]

Rationalization. Another device, which is sometimes so subtle in its expression that it is difficult to detect, is that by

[1] Henderson and Gillespie, *A Text-book of Psychiatry*, pp. 289 ff.
[2] See Chapter IV.

4

which the boy or girl unconsciously seeks an excuse for failing to adapt to life or to accept a new responsibility. At the most superficial level, and one which is in a large degree (though probably not entirely) conscious, this takes the form of self-justification and excuses for not following this or that unpleasant course of action. The refusal to adapt may however take place entirely on the unconscious level, and a physical symptom may develop which effectively supplies an excuse. 'Nervous breakdown', illness neurotically determined, hysterical symptoms like paralysis or vomiting for no apparent reason, and so on may all be traced to such unconscious causes.

To some or all of these devices in greater or lesser degree many adolescents resort. None of them is peculiar to adolescence, but any is likely to develop as a way of dealing with a situation which cannot be met and dealt with on the level of conscious adaptation; and as we have seen, adolescence is for very many a time of increased environmental and personal stress. They provide a temporary breathing-space in the struggle and, except for complete withdrawal or illness neurotically determined, constitute no undue abnormality. For healthy personal adjustment, however, they should be recognized for what they are and not be persisted in to the extent that they become a complete evasion of the task of adaptation. They are indicators that the balance between the adaptive capacity of the individual and the demands of life is not being maintained. Adolescents who persistently complain of being discriminated against, or who show abnormal fear or anxiety, or who boast of powers in a direction in which they are known to be inferior, or who plead vague ill-health for failing to do well at school, or who are excessively reserved or shy, are not developing healthily. Steps which lessen the pressure of the environment and which will show the way to healthy adaptation will do much to help; and, in serious cases, skilled psychological attention should be sought.

Compensation. Progress in the development of personality is not achieved by retreat. Inexorably, the boy or girl must go forward to adulthood, weaning the self from childish ways and bringing about an adjustment between the conscious and unconscious desires and the realities of life. Sometimes this is achieved by what the psychologist calls the mechanism of *compensation*, though whether it is adaptive or not depends very largely upon the form of activity to which it gives rise. As we have already pointed out earlier, day-dreams are a form of compensation; so may be boasting and lying; bravado or spitefulness, malicious lies, and downright delinquency which brings the youth into conflict with the law, may be activities prompted by a feeling of impotence or inferiority. More valuable is that form of compensation which consists in seeking success in a field different from the one which is feared. The girl who feels that she is not physically attractive may affect to despise good looks and cultivate a reputation for intellectual success. The boy who suffers from a physical handicap may despise 'flannell'd fools and muddied oafs' and turn to writing stories or verse of an heroic turn. One whose progress in ordinary school subjects is not good may compensate by becoming an authority on some subject which is so out of the way that there is no competition from contemporaries. Such compensations are not without the danger that they may be mistaken for the expression of genuine vocational talent. In other cases, the handicap or difficulty is recognized and a direct attack is made upon it. A physical defect, like clubfoot or a generally weak physique, may be met by a more than usually determined attempt to excel at sport. We have the example here of Sir Walter Scott who largely vanquished his physical handicap, and of Demosthenes who, tradition asserts, overcame a speech defect to become, not merely a normally competent speaker but a great orator. Examples of such over-compensations are difficult to detect; but we must attribute much of the bumptiousness, conceit, and excessive self-assurance shown by some adolescents to their attempts—mainly on a level scarcely conscious—to overcome a sense of anxiety or inferiority.

This process of compensation of which we have just been talking is a good example of the way in which some psychological tendencies may show themselves in the form of socially acceptable or of socially unacceptable behaviour, and may in fact be adaptive or maladaptive. This double aspect should be kept in mind as we turn to discuss other ways in which the adolescent meets the problems of growth. The processes which we have just been discussing generally serve the purpose of retreat: those we are about to discuss are generally aimed at a closer harmony with the environment. Their result in character formation will, however, depend largely upon the quality of the environmental stimulus and upon innate and developmental factors in the individual. In emotional growth more than in any other field is it true that one youth's meat is poison to another.

Imitation. The process of development and adaptation depends largely upon the incorporation into the individual self of ideas and ideals from the environment. As such it is basically the process of learning, and continues throughout life, every experience contributing its quota of modification to the character, and each having some meaning on the conscious and unconscious levels. We should be hard put to it ourselves to analyse even in the broadest detail the ways in which we have become what we are: but it is safe to say that the processes loosely termed *imitation* in popular language have played a very large part. Under this word, several important tendencies of the human mind are subsumed: and we may perhaps follow Nunn[1] in his distinction between *mimesis* ('the general tendency shown by an individual to take over from others their modes of action,

[1] *Education: Its Data and First Principles,* ch. xi (3rd ed., London, 1945). See also the brief discussion in Thouless, *General and Social Psychology* (London, 1937), pp. 313 ff.; McDougall, *Introduction to Social Psychology,* ch. iv (London, 1936); Stout and Mace, *Manual of Psychology,* bk. III, ch. iii (London, 1938).

feeling and thought') and *imitation* proper, which he limits to those aspects of mimesis in which the activity is conscious. Thus the infant who winks and smiles back at an adult[1] is probably exhibiting mimetic behaviour; but the adult or adolescent who studies the way in which a tennis player makes his strokes and then tries to copy the technique is imitating. Both of these tendencies may show themselves in action, feeling, and thought. Mimesis in the province of feeling is what McDougall calls the 'direct induction of emotion', and it is an important part of the effect which individuals have upon each other in social groups—clubs, schools, crowds, gangs, and the like. Mimesis in the province of thought is generally called *suggestion*—the unwilled adoption of another's ideas or of the ideas current in a particular social group, family, and so on. On the conscious level, there may be an attempt to imitate the outward appearances of emotion and thus to induce the state in oneself or to absorb the ideas of another by reasoned analysis.

Identification. Some of these processes are at work from the earliest years or even months of life. Though at first mimesis of simple actions is all that is observable, it is not long before it becomes complicated by elements of feeling and of thought and by conscious attempts to imitate. In its most complex form it becomes the tendency, seen at all ages after the earliest infancy, to play at being some striking personality in the environment. This tendency is closely linked with the fantasy life and we may adopt the term *identification* to cover the complex of conscious imitation and unconscious mimesis, of suggestion and of absorption of ideas and ideals, more or less consciously, which takes place when one person tries to appropriate to himself the ways and attitudes and something of the personality of another or to absorb the characteristics of an admired group.

At adolescence these processes are perhaps less obvious than

[1] Valentine, *The Psychology of Early Childhood*, p. 174 (London, 1942). See also the same book ch. x and xiii for a full discussion of the evidence for the innateness of suggestibility and mimesis.

in childhood but, if anything, more extensive in their influence on mental growth. The imitativeness of the child and his suggestibility are subject to limitations, and the first influences brought to bear upon him are mainly concrete and overt, proceeding from the immediate family environment. Strong identifications with parents, brothers, and sisters, imitations of mannerisms, behaviour, and modes of thinking, and highly suggestible attitudes to the words of adults and of other children are normal and important throughout infancy and childhood. The direction of attention and interest outwards at adolescence, from the family group to wider social circles—the school, the gang, the crowd, the world in general—at once broadens the range of models, and, by the very multiplicity of choice, blurs the hard outlines. Ignorance and lack of experience heighten suggestibility as does the prestige of the object of attention. Most adolescents are being brought into contact with many varying facets of adult life which they do not at first comprehend. Hence while the indentifications of the child seem intense, narrow, and relatively permanent, those of the normally developing adolescent may at times appear almost servile or a complex and wayward absorption of the superficial features of a group;[1] at other times an identification as intense as it is usually short-lived with an admired hero; at yet others a complete devotion to some abstract ideal.

If an adolescent is watched sympathetically, at least two progressive stages can be seen. At first the preoccupation with the model of the moment—individual, group, or set of ideals—is exclusive and followed frequently by indifference or strong contra-suggestibility, the function of which seems to be protective against complete submergence of the individuality. As the youth becomes more mature in the later teens, these identifications become less intense and more diffused, until the fully

[1] M. D. Vernon, 'Characteristic Motivation in the Activities of Schoolgirls,' B. Journ. P., vol. XXIX, pt. iii, January 1934.

developed and mature adult, although still susceptible to the influence of a personality stronger than his own, or swayed by the force of ideas, possesses an independence and individuality which protects him from the danger of complete disintegration on the one hand or servile imitation on the other; the swings of enthusiasm and indifference are less intense, imitation less potent and automatic, and suggestibility in very many directions counterbalanced by increased experience and knowledge.

Family Influences. The importance of these widening identifications on the development of personality is fundamental: and it is largely upon their quality in childhood and adolesecnce that the mature personality depends. In development up to adolescence, the greatest part is played by the parents and members of the immediate family circle.[1] From his father the little boy learns his first lessons in how to behave as a man, and in how women (as represented by his mother) should be treated. By identification with her mother, the little girl learns much of what is expected of her sex. Children appropriate to themselves and incorporate as part of their conscience—or as Freud calls it, their super-ego—the praise and blame bestowed upon them by the all-powerful adults in their circle. In play, fearful situations are re-enacted, fear-inspiring personages imitated, and so controlled. The ideals of the home are absorbed or *introjected* until they become an integral and inescapable part of the personality, against which the adult may rebel but to which he can never be indifferent. On the parents' attitudes, on the relationship between their spoken opinions and actual behaviour, and upon the child's interpretation of each family situation as it arises, will depend day by day the moulding of his growing self. The little girl sent to the door to tell an unwelcome visitor that Mummy is not at home is being apprenticed to deceit. The boy continually berated by an exacting

[1] The best discussion of the importance of family influences in the development of the individual is to be found in the previously cited book by Flügel, *A Psychoanalytic Study of the Family.*

father for failure at school is learning a bitter sense of his own inferiority. Parental quarrels have a profound effect upon immature minds and family strife is one of the principal causes of mental conflict in children. Similarly the child whose individuality is respected, who sees before him a family in which each has recognized duties as well as privileges, is learning valuable lessons in wider fields of social co-operation.

It is likely that much of this absorption of family attitudes proceeds at an unconscious level and that the influences of the home are assimilated without even rudimentary critical evaluation. Their influence is the more powerful because the more intense and narrow. Furthermore, attitudes of others as they issue in behaviour have more effect than do precepts; for, while it seems that the best and most moral opinions can be instilled by training, they can coexist in the same personality with behaviour that falls lamentably short of excellence. It has for example been found that on many moral problems the opinions of delinquent and non-delinquent children are determined as much by school or home teaching as by anything else,[1] but that behaviour is dictated by mental attitudes, sometimes of compulsive force, nurtured in the family situation or at least by immediate environment. Our children are inclined more to do as we do, than as we say.

Lessening Influence of Parents. At adolescence, this intense ascendancy of the parents and of the family tends to lessen. Home should still supply a background and a safe retreat, a place where one is valued and wanted; but it should no longer be all in all. Wider experience and contact with other groups —the office, the club, the houses of a widening circle of friends —and a greater range of travel should combine with the increased self-awareness and interest in social life to ensure emancipation. For a time, perhaps, with some youths, there may be an increase in the influence of the parent of opposite

[1] Burt, *The Young Delinquent,* pp. 409 ff.

sex.[1] The girl may turn to her father as a model of what men should be and the boy to his mother for his idea of woman; both see in the relationships between their parents a pattern of married life which represents their most intimate information on a subject which is beginning to loom as a problem.[2] In cases where parental relationships are happy there is no danger in this, and the influence of the parent on the subsequent love life of a child will be good. Where, however, there is frustration and unhappiness in the parents' married life—even if this has not caused an open breach—the mother or father is all too apt to seek a substitute outlet in the growing child. An adolescent who succumbs to a more than usually strong tie or identification with the parent may be prevented by it from making an adequate adjustment to a wife or husband later on. It is from such involvements that situations arise in which the wife is continually critical of her husband or in which the husband makes disparaging comparisons of his wife with his mother. In other cases the child turns quite away from home and reacts violently against all the suggestions of his parents. The boy may delight in embracing extreme opinions in opposition to his father, the girl rejects even the gentlest of maternal hints. Such phases, if not allowed to become a storm centre of angry reproaches and recriminations, pass, to be succeeded eventually in early man- or womanhood by an affection based on mutual respect. If such youths are not tactfully handled, their bid for independence may be balked, leaving a docile apron-stringed adult; or may flame into open revolt which separates parent and child for the rest of their lives.

Psychological Weaning. Progress is achieved at adolescence by a steady weaning from parental influence, a weaning which may be compared with weaning in infancy and which is apt to be fraught with as much emotional upset. The infant kept too long dependent upon the breast and the adolescent too

---

[1] See Chapter IV.   [2] See Chapter IV, *Fantasy.*

dependent upon parents present pitiful pictures of strain. Conflicts arising in infancy at weaning time may be reanimated at adolescence in a form more difficult to deal with; and the anxieties of the child which were shown in tantrums and screaming fits may become phases of acute melancholy, loss of appetite, attempted suicide, inability to leave home, neurotically determined illness, and so on, in adolescence. Some parents, especially mothers whose whole life has been devoted to their children, find it difficult to concede them independence even by degrees. Their influence is continually being exerted against outside persons, by subtle deprecation, by continued interference, or by playing upon a filial sense of duty. Such a mother as is portrayed in *Dear Octopus* is a drag upon the free development of her children. If child-bearing and child-rearing has been a career, it is hard to see one's occupation go, but it must be recognized that the process is as necessary as weaning in infancy, and that with wisdom and foresight it can be compassed without upset, and without enduring loss of affection.

What has been said of parents is, in lesser, degree true also of other persons in the environment. Teachers, club leaders, clergymen, all who come into contact with young people are likely to be taken as models. From what they do and are, attitudes will be absorbed and the values of adult life learned. The attachments to grown-ups formed in the *early* teens are particularly liable to be passionate—the intense hero-worship of the boy, the burning 'crush' of the girl.[1] Such situations are fraught with danger for the young, not so much from the chance of overt homosexual experience, which is relatively uncommon, but from the likelihood that, instead of encouraging the callow youth to achieve independence, the adult will seek an outlet for his or her own frustrations in the uncritical love of the growing girl or boy.

[1] A good study of a rather extreme 'crush' with fatal results forms the theme of Christa Winsloe's *Children in Uniform*.

Independence. Independence can be encouraged in many ways. In the home, a room of one's own, an increasing share in the family councils, the right to control more and more of one's personal expenditure, choice and purchase of clothes, a decreasing parental insistence on knowing all the movements and activities of the adolescent, an increasing insistence—gentle, firm, and progressive—on the duty of taking important decisions for oneself and abiding by their consequences, a respect on the part of parents for the reticence and for the opinions of their children, and a realization on our part that what we are apt to term experience is frequently only the rather melancholy record of our failures and mistakes: all these help the normal drive towards individual emancipation. Outside the home, personal influences are more diffuse and less intensive. Friends, the school, the club, all have their part to play; and all should foster experiment with living and allow the adolescent to try out the many potential selves which are inherent in all of us. Responsibility for others, service to a community, self-government, identification with a cause which is valued in the adult world, a feeling of being needed for one's own sake, are things which can be implicit in a good youth club, school society, or pre-service organization. The approval of a group acts as a steadying influence on the immature personality, supporting and propping it until a reasonable measure of independence is achieved; practice in a wider world of behaviour than the home, allows the development of potentialities which might otherwise lie dormant; and the clash and conflict of desires among equals and contemporaries is a microcosm of what will be met with in the adult world.

Culture. There is a third great field offering identifications, models, precepts, and examples, many of them in conflict with the narrower range of experience of home, school, and club. The growing intellectual ability of the adolescent, the wider range of interests, the sharpened introspective powers, the stir and movement of emotions, and the comparative perfection of educational techniques imparted in preceding years, open up the whole culture of the race enshrined in art and in literature. The youth may, as never before, become 'the heir of all the ages'.

How far these influences are brought to bear, particularly in the late teens, is a matter of intellectual quality, of the personal influence of adults, and of educational opportunity. With some the merest superficiality of cheap novelettes is their only contact with a wider world than home and street. It is not surprising that, to such, the use of cosmetics, smoking, jive and jitterbug, tentative sexual experiment, and a love of continual excitement represent the values of the adult world and the signs of maturity. For very many, the screen is a complete school of personality, offering instruction, in the most readily assimilable forms, in details of dress, hair-style, manners, behaviour, language, love-making, and the whole conduct of life.[1] To others more favoured by innate intelligence and by educational opportunities, all that is valuable and permanent in our culture is opened up. Emotional developments, particularly the new energy derived from sex interests, make great literature a storehouse of keenly felt experience. The classics of our tongue, the huge body of philosophic and erotic poetry, drama with its portrayal of emotional conflict and concentrated energy of living, may become a powerful influence in spiritual progress. The ideals offered by religion, politics, philosophy are tried out, embraced perhaps for a time, consciously absorbed or rejected, debated, criticized, and compared with the practice of their professors. Widening social experience and the expanding boundaries of the mind, press the individual forward to experiment, to try the new self out in a variety of roles. If the models presented are worthy ones, these experiments will be of untold value. If they are shallow, conflicting, empty of social significance, we shall get the picture so irately drawn of modern

[1] See Chapter V.

youth by the tetchy letter-writers to the Press. The behaviour of adolescents is a heightened picture of the adult world as they see it. It may be a caricature: it is none the less a shrewd criticism. The virtue or villainy we teach them they will execute and it goes hard but they better the instruction.

Variety of Types. The numerous patterns offered by an advanced civilization such as ours, though many of them may be in conflict, offer advantages as well as sources of stress and friction. There are few intellectual and emotional types who cannot find rest somewhere within a group. Some few aberrations from the norm, such as overt homosexuality, are tolerated at hardly any level; others only in certain cliques or social strata: yet it may be said that the healthy extrovert of boundless physical energy and the quietist, the philistine, the aesthete, the man of action, the man of ideas, the constructor, the pioneer, the poet, the visionary, the artist, the critic, the cynic, and the individualist; all these and a thousand more can at length find themselves in harmony with others of their kind. The multiplicity of pattern makes the finding of a self at adolescence difficult and is paid for by a greater incidence of minor maladjustments and perhaps by neurosis. It complicates the search for happiness and harmony, but it offers for all a greater possibility of self-realization, and since one individual may be a member of many groups simultaneously, social, political, religious, regional—to each of which something of the self is given and from which sustenance is drawn—it makes for rich variety in the adult character. The duty of society towards the new generation is to foster individual choice and variation, to make smooth the way to identification with suitable groups, and to see that, by its own tolerance of aberrations which are not socially undesirable, the youth reaches maturity with the minimum of frustration and maladaptation.

Aspects of the Self. We have been talking so far as if the self at maturity were a unitary thing. In one sense this is true. In another sense the remark of William James that a man has as many selves as there are groups to which he belongs is also true. It is perhaps best to think of various aspects of personality being at one time dominant and at another subordinate. We are all acquainted with the man who appears quite different in personality in his own home from in the office. Few of us are the same in all circumstances and indeed such an inflexibility might just as much imply a pathological weakness of character as too great a variability. It is also true to say that in some directions our adjustments to life are more successful than in others. A good adjustment to marriage for example may coexist with unhappiness in one's vocation and a severe crisis of doubt in religion; or a woman happy in her job, certain of her philosophy of life, may find heterosexual adjustments a continual source of strain. Such conflicts, unless they become insistent, although they may cause unhappiness, need not interfere with efficiency and harmony in other directions, and indeed a successful adjustment of, say, the social self may do much to compensate for conflict in the sexual or vocational spheres. Equally obviously the desirable thing is adjustment at all points.

Integration. The adolescent then is proceeding from the relatively simple self of childhood adjusted to home and to the demands of school to a complex and faceted self which has to make compromise with a social environment compartmented in many more directions. The youth is putting off childish things and ceasing to be dependent, physically or intellectually, on his parents and those adults, like teachers, who stand in a parental relation to him. This independence has to be achieved by all of us and in all the major fields of human activity, social, vocational, and sexual. Beyond everything, however, and in all the spheres of living, something like a unity has to be established. The keystone of this unity will be a master sentiment concerning the self—embracing ideas and adjustments built up from experience, and taking full cognizance of strengths and weaknesses both in relation to one's fellows and to the demands of the environment. Thus adolescence may be likened to an emotional weaning, during which the uncompromising egotism of infancy and childhood has to be merged with altruistic impulses and ideals to form the foundation of a mature outlook. Temperament, intelligence, instinctive life, ingrained habits of response built up from earliest days, the influences of home and school, of parents, brothers, sisters, and companions, have to be moulded to adapt to the less protected and more exacting adult world. Little wonder is it that, at times, Jack or Jill is 'changeable, longing and liking; proud, fantastical, apish, shallow, inconstant; full of tears, full of smiles, for every passion something, and for no passion truly anything'. Such instability may be the sign of a character in flux. It offers possibly the last opportunity for shaping the emergent personality. The wise parent or teacher stands a little aloof, ready with affectionate understanding, ready with help and a timely word of encouragement or idealism when life seems to be hard. In our own way each of us has to work out our own salvation. No one can find it for us and a solution that comes readymade is apt to fail in a crisis. The best that the older generation can do is to see that worthy materials are at hand, worthy objects for identification, worthy causes to serve and great ideals. We can also see that the fundamental needs of the developing mind are not frustrated; and that the faith and fire of the young do not meet with the heartbreaking cynicism of the old.

CHAPTER III

LOVE AND FRIENDSHIP

Sex Development. The growth and integration of character of which we have just been speaking may be profoundly affected by the adjustments which are made in the sex life. We have emphasized before that developments in this sphere, which, for many, are a marked feature of the teens, cannot be traced *directly* to the action of the sex hormones, or even to the attainment of puberty. Sex expression is very largely a matter of cultural regulation; and, even within the broad pattern prevailing in a society such as ours, there exist wide differences between one group and another. Boys and girls in single-sex boarding-schools, for example, are in a profoundly different mental atmosphere with regard to sex from their contemporaries in, say, co-educational day schools, or factory workshops. Overt sex behaviour such as flirtation, the writing of love letters, marked shyness in the presence of members of the opposite sex, and so on may be delayed in the boy or girl from the segregated boarding-school until two or three years after puberty has been attained. In the co-educational school they may appear only in a very mild form and perhaps be condemned by public opinion. The influence of companions in other environments may induce a precocious interest even before puberty; and the presence of young adults in a factory workshop may give a sudden, and not necessarily desirable, mature turn to the sex interests of an adolescent worker.

Such environmental differences are contributory factors to the wide individual differences in the age incidence of the rise of interest in the opposite sex and in the form taken by the first advances. Both in the strength of the innate impulses themselves and in those influences, personal and environmental, which modify them from birth onwards, the differcnces between individuals, even in one comparatively unified group, are wide. Nevertheless, the attainment of puberty is the central psychological and physiological fact upon which many attitudes of the adolescent and of society in general tend to precipitate; and fundamentally the problem for all boys and girls as they pass from childhood to adulthood is that of making an accommodation between a biological drive which has perhaps intensified markedly in the teens and the demands of the particular social setting in which they find themselves.

In this development we can distinguish roughly certain broad phases, shown by many boys and girls in our society. The early stages are described in a whole colloquial vocabulary of terms and phrases—'puppy love', 'necking', 'petting', 'crush', 'pash', and a great many more—hostile, indulgent, ironic, or merely descriptive. Later comes the canalizing of affection and passion, romantic first love with its humility and boldness, its depreciation of the self and overvaluation of another. Through time or change, distance or accident, such first love usually fades: it is seen as an illusion, and not 'the marriage of true minds'. It is followed by others, and in such experiments the youth perfects and matures his own personality and learns to look beyond the 'phantom of delight' to the

> . . . creature not too bright or good
> For human nature's daily food.

Some overvaluation of the sexual object is probably present even in the love of the most developed adult, but it is only when the young man and woman can maturely recognize their own and each other's true worth that they are ready to choose a mate, to make that monogamous adjustment to another which Thouless[1] regards as probably an innate pattern in man. The

[1] *General and Social Psychology*, p. 159.

5

change of the teens is from the self-centred, self-regarding world of the child to a more selfless preoccupation with the wellbeing of another. When the teens have passed and marriage is no longer an *egoisme à deux*, the protective and altruistic impulses which form an important component part[1] of the emotions related to parenthood but which are present in the noblest human love should again widen in scope to embrace the growing family and broader social groupings.

Importance of Integration. The successful achievement of this cycle of development depends upon an integration of the emotional and physical aspects of the sex life. It is an unhappy fact that, under modern conditions, many fail to achieve to the full the potentialities of this development, with an inestimable loss of happiness to themselves and of value to society. Freud's view that maldevelopment in the sex life is the cause of *all* neurotic illness has been challenged by experience of psychological breakdown in war;[2] and it has been shown that the frustration of any powerful innate drive—for example those of self-assertion or self-preservation—may lead to mental disaster. To the adolescent, however, making adjustments in many fields, sex is frequently the most devouring problem, a new and inexplicable power for which he is unprepared by previous experience, and the expression of which is hedged about with secrecy and prohibition. A maladjustment in this field, developing either before or during adolescence, may turn awry many associated currents of the emotional life and seriously hinder, if not thwart altogether, the establishment of a unified personality well adapted to daily life.

The Oedipus Complex. Much of the ease or difficulty with which the problem is faced will be dependent upon the previous

---

[1] McDougall, *Introduction to Social Psychology*, pp. 56, 438 (23rd edn., London, 1936).
[2] McDougall, *Abnormal Psychology, passim* (London, 1926). E. Miller (Ed.), *The Neuroses in War*, Ch. i and xi (London, 1940); H. Crichton Miller (Ed.), *Functional Nerve Disease* (Oxford), contributions by Prideaux and McDougall.

life experience of the individual boy or girl; and we may perhaps consider here briefly the conception of sexuality and sex development held by the psycho-analytic school. Freud and his followers hold that the sex adjustments of the adolescent and adult are dominated in a peculiar and universal way by experience in infancy and early life. They suggest that the gratification found by the infant in suckling, defaecation, thumb-sucking, attention from the mother, and the like, is erotic and psychologically closely akin to the sensuous pleasure of adult sexuality. According to this interpretation, the first love object is the child's own body and especially the external orifices. As minister to this form of gratification, the mother becomes the recipient of a peculiarly intense love. In the little boy, this persists; and collateral with it goes a jealousy and hatred of the father because of his rights to the affection of the beloved mother. On the unconscious level the boy wishes to be rid of his father and to enjoy a *literally* incestuous possession of his mother. Opposing this however is the power of his father, and the feeling of love and respect for him. This, the social taboo on the incestuous relationship which he desires, and the fear of castration for overtly sexual behaviour, unite to repress the sexuality of infancy and lead to a period of latency which lasts until immediately prior to puberty. This early love for the mother, and the mingled sexual jealousy, hatred, fear and love for the father, constitute the Oedipus complex of which so much is heard in psycho-analytic writings and which is held to dominate the later love life as well as being the nuclear complex of the neuroses and the beginnings of religion, ethics, and even of society and art.

With the girl, the development is held to be more tortuous. In the female infant the same auto-erotic phase occurs, and the same direction of *libido*, or intense desire, onto the mother. In some obscure way (Freud suggests it is because fathers favour their daughters) this early fixation on the mother changes in direction during infancy, and the little girl comes unconsciously to wish to be rid of her mother and to enjoy exclusive sexual possession of her father. This, to correspond with the Oedipus complex, has been named the Electra complex.

The supposed importance of this conception to a study of adolescence lies in the effect which these early infantile complexes are alleged to have on sexual adjustments later. It is suggested that, especially in the case of the boy, the fixation on the mother may dominate his love choice in one of two ways. He may fall in love with a woman resembling his mother as closely as possible—even, in the detail of age, choosing a mate much older than himself. Or, if the feelings of unconscious guilt attached to his repressed incestuous longing for his mother are too great, he may be influenced by them to choose a woman as unlike his mother as possible. In the girl similar and complementary effects of the Electra complex are supposed to be traceable.[1]

Evidence. This is a bald statement of the tenets of the psychoanalytic school, who adduce in support of their thesis much evidence derived from their own studies of admittedly abnormal adults and children. There is little statistical fact one way or the other; and the objective evidence which we do possess[2] suggests that the universality of the Oedipus complex is far from proved. Nor does there seem to be much evidence for the specifically *sexual* nature of the delight of young children in thumb-sucking, exploring their own bodies, suckling, defaecation and the like. The work of Moll and Havelock Ellis[3] seems, further, to dispose

[1] It is impossible to give more than a selection from the vast Freudian literature which has grown up around these topics. The reader is referred for an elementary treatment to Flügel, *Introduction to Psycho-analysis* (London, 1932), or Crichton-Miller, *Psycho-analysis and its Derivatives* (London, 1933). A more advanced treatment is found in the works of Freud himself, or in Jones, *Papers on Psychoanalysis* (4th edn., London, 1938). For an example of the application of extreme Freudian views to the study of adolescence the reader should turn to Mannin, *Commonsense and the Adolescent* (London, 1937).

[2] Valentine, *The Psychology of Early Childhood*, ch. xvii, 'The Supposed Oedipus Complex'.

[3] Moll, *The Sexual Life of the Child* (London, 1912); Havelock Ellis, *The Psychology of Sex*, vol. I (Philadelphia, 1928).

of the idea of a period of *latency* in the sex life between infancy and puberty. The fact of the matter appears to be, as Valentine[1] concludes after a full discussion of a wide range of data, that 'any sexual sensations and impulses are only of a very mild kind from early infancy at least until a year or two before puberty'.

Thus, until eleven or twelve with most children, the sex instinct and the sex sentiment—the biological drive and the emotional complex of feeling and experience—are imperfect and probably largely independent. Neither normally occupies a central position, physically or emotionally, in the life of the child. Deliberate erotic stimulation in childhood, too great an emotional demand by either parent, sexual shocks, and the like will undoubtedly disturb the development of this 'proto-sexuality' as Thouless[2] calls it, and produce conflicts which come strongly to the surface with the access of sexual energy at puberty. In some, perhaps in many, cases of neurosis, an Oedipus or Electra complex, or something very like it, may be a factor of importance.

Sources of Conflict. With physiological maturation, however, sex assumes a dominating place in the emotional life; and it is doubtful whether in a modern civilization and without an adequate sex education, any boy or girl achieves an integration between the physical and emotional aspects of sex in the teens without some conflict and struggle. To the girl, first menstruation, and to the boy, the first ejaculation whether accidental or the result of self-manipulation, comes as something of a shock. The close juxtaposition or identity of sexual and excretory organs—themselves associated with nursery conflicts over training in cleanliness—tends to link the new physiological activity with ideas of dirtiness and shame. This may be the

---

[1] *The Psychology of Early Childhood*, p. 351. Chapters xvii and xviii of this book contain, so far as I know, the only truly objective evidence on these vexed questions.

[2] op. cit., p. 171.

more upsetting since sex is a subject on which few young people care to confide in adults who have in the past met direct questions with evasions or embarrassed fairy tales.

Masturbation. More usually, however, conflict arises, in boys especially, around masturbation. Infantile explorations of the body sooner or later find the genitals, stimulation of which, possibly even in the earliest years, gives pleasure. This pleasant occupation the infant or child finds discouraged by stern disapprobation, even by threats, for, in the mind of many adults, still lingers the unhappy misconception that childhood self-manipulation is a stigma of degeneracy. With puberty, physical sexual tension rises and research indicates that masturbation is practised by between 70 and 99 per cent. of boys, with a peak incidence in the early teens.[1] In girls, largely because the tension is less noticeably directed to the genitals by perceptible local changes, *conscious* masturbatory processes may be less common. Prior to puberty such practices are probably unaccompanied by sexual imagery, but later, at least in the boy, erotic fantasy soon provokes a genital reaction which makes the connexion unmistakable to consciousness. The social attitude which rates the physical side of sex as something shamefully secret, the well-intentioned but dangerously misleading books which spread the superstition that 'self-abuse is the high road to insanity', and the teachings of religion that the cravings of the flesh are sinful and that total abstinence is possible, all unite to provoke a crisis of painful self-revulsion.

It is now generally agreed by psychological and medical opinion[2] that while very excessive masturbation may cause marked nervous and physical exhaustion, even frequent indulgence is unlikely to have serious or lasting affects *in itself.*

[1] Hall, *Adolescence*, vol. i, p. 435; Bühler, *From Birth to Maturity*, pp. 182–4 (London, 1937), following Freidjung, Boenheim, Hirschfeld, Meirowsky, and others. See also Havelock Ellis, *The Psychology of Sex*, vol. i; Dickenson and Beam, *The Single Woman* (London, 1934).

[2] Read, *Struggles of Male Adolescence*, p. 158 (London, 1928); Havelock Ellis, op. cit., vol. i.

The emotional reaction to it provoked by ignorance and wrong training is, however, a serious danger. Feelings of unworthiness, hours of lonely and unavailing struggle, intense moral conflict, anxiety lest outward signs should lead to discovery, and a guilty sense of uncleanness, may lead straight to psychological disaster. Fear of insanity has led some adolescents to suicide, and more to suicidal thoughts. One boy covers the secret loss of self-respect by boisterous self-assertion; another, by an obsessional preoccupation with cleanliness; in yet others, moods of withdrawal, gloom, and depression persist for days. For most, though the crises are keen, they pass eventually with increasing maturity and especially with growing knowledge. Apart from neurosis the serious dangers for development lie in the possibility that sex expression, even in marriage, may become fixed at the auto-erotic level;[1] or that, regarding the practice as filthy, the adolescent may dissociate in his mind the physical aspects of love from those based on affection and esteem.[2] *She Stoops to Conquer* is an interesting comic study of such a serious psychological situation.

Sex Consciousness. Studies of adolescents in many different countries have revealed that sex consciousness begins about the age of twelve, and that some kind of enlightenment on the topic, usually from playmates or corrupt domestics, is received before that.[3] Such initiations frequently come as a shock of repugnance or disgust, and remain as a horrid guilty secret. In early adolescence, this half-knowledge becomes more highly charged with emotion, forming a factor in the friendships of boys and girls, and in the formation of secret societies with vaguely obscene ceremonial. Ethel Mannin describes one such to which she belonged and in which 'it' was discussed and obscene rhymes

[1] Read, op. cit., p. 158; Jones, op. cit., pp. 396 ff.
[2] Flügel, *Psycho-Analytic Study of the Family*, pp. 111-2.
[3] Hughes, cited by Hollingworth, *Handbook of Child Psychology*, p. 887; Burgess, cited by Partridge, *The Social Psychology of Adolescence*, p. 171; Carnivet, 'Enquête sur l'initiation sexuelle', *Arch. de Psychologie*, vol. xxiii, No. 91, January 1932.

recited.[1] Another came within the author's knowledge in which the principal occupation was undressing in secret places. Often an acute awareness of *double entendre* induces an obsessional avoidance of common words for a time, or the teacher will notice an inexplicable tension in a class of fourteen-year-olds. Dictionaries, medical works, and encyclopaedias are surreptitiously consulted by youths in search of information with which a wise sex education would have provided them. Two fifteen-year-olds of my acquaintance spent a whole long day at the public library investigating the sex life of the whale in vain —a laboriously indirect way of acquiring knowledge!

So far the developments and conflicts we have been discussing represent what might be called the more egocentric aspects of sex. Throughout adolescence and even in adulthood they may form the background, the accompaniment as it were, to the social aspects of the sex life and the interrelation between the two is subtle and profound. In this sphere too there are probably wide divergencies between the sexes. The research referred to in Chapter II suggested that with girls, interest is early concentrated upon the behavioural aspects of the sex life, whereas, at least in his early teens, the boy is still preoccupied with finding out facts and with conflict over auto-erotic practices. As with all generalizations about adolescents, however, this is subject to a multitude of individual exceptions, and the field in which conflict arises—even the presence or absence of conflict—will depend upon previous life experience, the stage of physical and emotional maturity reached in relation to contemporaries, and the kind and extent of the enlightenment possessed by the individual both as to the facts and as to the emotional experiences connected with sex.

Parental Influence. With this reservation in mind, we may

[1] Deutsch, op. cit., p. 147; Mannin, *Commonsense and the Adolescent*, pp. 150-2; Eden and Cedar Paul (trans.), *A Young Girl's Diary*, pp. 22-5 (New York, 1936); McCurdy, *Problems in Dynamic Psychology*, p. 316 (Cambridge and New York, 1923).

trace in broad outline the growth of the more outwardly directed emotions of the sex life. In the early stages this seems to take the form of a generally sharpened awareness of others. One of the first signs may be a profound change in the balance of the influence wielded by father and mother. For example, among the students studied by Valentine[1] 54 per cent. of men and 39 per cent. of women reported a decline during adolescence in the father's influence and 44 per cent. of men and 25 per cent. of women a decline of the mother's. On the other hand, the influence of the father increased with 45 per cent. of the men and 27 per cent. of the women, and the influence of the mother with 40 per cent. of the men and 42 per cent. of the women.

In general, however, the ascendancy of the parents, love for whom is frequently complicated by clashes with their authority and disillusion as to their infallibility, tends to decline. There may be a feeling that 'they don't understand' which may amount to a fierce, but usually secret, resentment against one or both, often without adequate foundation in fact. One youth of my acquaintance nourished the fantasy, only half-held, that his mother was trying to poison him with some peach jam, which he resolutely refused to eat. Burt[2] records examples of fantasies in which the child believes that its father or mother are not the real parents, a circumstance most likely to arise when there is any mystery attaching to either parent or when one is dead or has married again.

Friendships. The close dependence upon the parents which is characteristic of the child, is replaced by a growing outflow of emotion to contemporaries. We have seen already something of this tendency away from the home and towards a wider social environment in the two groups of adolescents described in Chapter II; and Valentine's[3] older and more highly selected

[1] Valentine, 'Adolescence and Some Problems of Youth Training', *B. Journ. Ed. P.*, vol. xiii, pt. 2, June 1943.

[2] Burt, *Young Delinquent*, pp. 370-4, 385 ff., 484-5; and especially pp. 548-50.

[3] loc. cit.

student group recorded an intensification of the impulse to seek the company of others in 60 per cent. of cases. Partly this is due, no doubt, to the need of the growing personality for support from its contemporaries; but in part, too, it is to be ascribed to emotions which will later canalize on a single object of love. Equally characteristic of the period is a tendency to form passionate attachments to members of the same sex. The object of this affection may be a contemporary who becomes a 'best friend' with whom everything is done, all secrets shared, and all tastes held in common. It is not at all uncommon to find, among fourteen- or fifteen-year-old girls particularly, inseparable couples who obstinately refuse even to go from one end of a building to another on a momentary errand unaccompanied. When circumstances force them apart, they write to each other daily, as do the young ladies in Jane Austen's *Love and Freindship* or Rita and Hella in a *Young Girl's Diary*. If a rival appears on the scene, they suffer acute pangs of jealousy; and they frequently indulge in a lovers' ritual of parting. Two fifteen-year-old girls known to the writer never separated for the night without emotional embraces, kisses, and the recitation of 'Be good, sweet maid, and let who will be clever . . .'

Such friendships are equally characteristic of the adolescence of boys, with whom, however, they are usually less overtly emotional, less exclusive of others, and less subject to jealousy. Iovetz-Tereshchenko[1] cites a diary description by an adolescent of the sudden dawn of such a friendship with a 'first long talk' about the sciences and history, and the emotional perturbation which followed it. Sometimes the friendship between two boys forms a nucleus around which grows up a group with kindred interests. One such came within the writer's knowledge. J. and P. became firm friends in the sixth form at school, though superficially their interests were very different. J. was absorbed in botany, bird life, and the biological sciences generally; P. was

[1] *Friendship—Love in Adolescence*, pp. 70–4 (London, 1936).

pursuing a course in the humanities with interests mainly literary and artistic. Each however not merely tolerated but shared as a junior partner in the pursuits of the other. In common they had a love of walking and went on long expeditions together, each pursuing his own or seconding the other's occupations. Round them grew an outer group of youths with something in common with one or both. This larger group spent hours discussing political, philosophical, religious, or social problems, listening to music, and so on. The competition of heterosexual interests eventually broke up the 'crowd', but the intimacy of J. and P. persisted through separation, marriage, and parenthood to be a steady formative influence throughout their lives.

This relative permanency of adolescent friendships—especially of those formed in the late teens—is in strong contrast to the ephemeral companionships of childhood which rarely survive separation or differential development. Evidence of their universality is provided by Wheeler,[1] three-quarters of whose student group and rather more of whose workers reported the formation of important friendships in the teens. Their influence in the development of personality cannot be overstated. Such attractions may be an important causative factor in crime,[2] or, by the clash of viewpoints and interests within a steady framework of affection, they may act as a training-ground of respect for the integrity of another's personality and help to formulate the adolescent philosophy of life.

'*Crushes*' *and Hero-worship*. Not infrequently the attachment is not the friendship of contemporaries, but springs up between a younger and an older youth of either sex, or between an adolescent and an adult. Such 'crushes' are usually more ephemeral, though during their brief span, they may be deeply, even dangerously, passionate. Unlike attractions between

---

[1] *The Adventure of Youth*, p. 74 (London, 1945).
[2] Burt, op. cit., pp. 129, 607.

equals, the psychological causes are markedly different in each of the partners. For the younger, the attraction to a senior or to an adult may be a transition between emotional dependence upon a parent and adjustment to contemporaries of the same or opposite sex. For the elder the uncritical devotion of the younger may satisfy pride, appeal to protective impulses; or, in the case of the older boy, something feminine in his junior may be reminiscent of girls to whom he is not yet adjusted.

In boys' schools, especially where segregation is strictly enforced as in boarding-schools, attractions between adolescent seniors and pre-pubertal juniors are by no means infrequent, often as the result of a school play in which young lads take female parts. For the most part these attractions are brief, lasting a few days or weeks only, and are marked by a desire for the company of the other, jealousy at interference, and romantic emotional devotion.

With girls the 'crush' or 'pash' is often more one-sided and more usually directed to an adult—the gym. or games mistress, or women of an athletic, perhaps slightly mannish, build. The accompanying emotion is intense and an epidemic of 'g.p.s.' may spread until a school or camp is entirely dis-organized. Adolescent girls write verses, perform labours of love, bring flowers and expensive presents, cherish photographs, lie in wait for the object of their love who becomes the centre of a realm of fantasy. 'My last and most painful crush,' writes a graduate student in a confidential essay, 'was the unfortunate gym-mistress. If I should meet her on my way to school, as I daily planned to do, I was so overcome I was almost incapable of speech. As I was games captain at the time, I had many opportunities of being with her which I was quick to seize upon. Often of an afternoon I would stay behind to paint hockey balls, or blow up netballs or have a general tidy-up of the games room. If she were away from school for even a day I was ridiculously disappointed. Always I was imagining myself injured on the hockey field or in the gymnasium so that I might be lifted up by her. There was perhaps in this an unconscious desire for physical contact, although I never felt this desire with a boy friend.'

Such attractions are more common in segregated schools and do not seem to occur with such violence where normal hetero-sexual objects are available. Co-education diminishes the tendency, though the less intense and more valuable projection of ideals on to another, which is the basis of hero-worship, persists. In such passionate attractions between members of the same sex, and particularly between boys, the danger of actual homosexual experience and of consequent shock or continued perversion is always implicit but greatly exaggerated. Where it does occur the danger lies in the guilty conflict engendered in the sensitive mind rather than in permanent inversion. The wise adult is unobtrusively watchful and avoids if possible dramatic intervention which may precipitate the very crisis it seeks to avoid. Distraction by alternative activities is the most sensible course; and the grown-up recipient of the ardent affection of an adolescent girl, by matter-of-fact treatment, can use her influence to kindle interests and form the malleable character.

Flirtation. The formation of such intense friendships, crushes, and hero-worship may be contemporary with or just antecedent to a rising interest in the opposite sex. Of the group of adolescents studied by the writer 70 per cent. reported increased heterosexual interests since 13, a finding confirmed by Valentine's[1] older group and by Wheeler's.[2] The rise of such interest, however, shows great individual variation. Kuhlen and Lee[3] found that, although boys and girls from 11 to 17½ chose the opposite sex as companions in an increasing

[1] loc. cit.
[2] loc. cit.
[3] 'Personality Characteristics and Social Acceptability in Adolescence', *Journ. Ed. Psych.*, vo l. xxxiv, No. 6, September 1943.

proportion as they grew older, even at 17 a quarter of the group still clung to their own sex.

At first this attraction may be generalized, embracing a group of the opposite sex. In his study of adolescent diaries, Iovetz-Tereshchenko[1] reveals what he calls a phase of 'pan-love for schoolgirls'—an emotional preoccupation with girls of a certain age. During this comparatively early stage, there frequently is a series—breath-takingly kaleidoscopic sometimes—of flirtations. The adolescent appears, as St. Augustine says of himself, to be 'more in love with loving than anything else', and Hamilton[2] found that his subjects reported an average of seven love affairs. Though ephemeral, however, the feelings aroused may be intense and 'the burning rods of jealousy' are keenly felt. These affairs are often the subject of confidences between friends of the same sex, and the whole emotional state is vaguely and allusively referred to as 'that'—itself a symptom of the shyness and reserve which accompany these early heterosexual approaches.[3]

Withdrawal. This phase of flirtation is sometimes followed by one of withdrawal. The short periods of segregation enforced by many primitive societies around puberty suggest that it may be biologically determined. The psychological explanation has been put forward that such a phase of withdrawal is a defensive retreat from the overwhelming increase in the sex drive and that it gives time for the new desires to be integrated and for the personality to learn control.

Serious attachments. Later, the love life takes a more mature turn. Generalized attraction and flirtation give way to more serious attachments. At first, especially if love for the parents has been very marked or if the weaning process has not worked itself out, the adolescent boy or girl may fall in love with a person much older and more mature. Not infrequently such

[1] op. cit., pp. 140 ff.
[2] *A Research in Marriage* (New York, 1929).
[3] Vide Meredith, *The Ordeal of Richard Feverell*, chap. xiv.

affairs culminate in marriage and, unless the element of parental fixation is too strong, can be successful. Some such unconscious motive may have lain behind the marriages of Dr. Johnson and Shakespeare, each of whom married a woman considerably his senior. Women tend to choose mates somewhat older than themselves rather more frequently than do men, a tendency fostered by economic conditions and not undesirable biologically. For a man the choice of a mate markedly older than himself is undesirable both biologically and economically, and a great difference in age may lead to psychological difficulties in middle life.

More usually this love for an older person is an intermediate adjustment, followed, in the late teens and early twenties, by attractions to closer contemporaries, one of which culminates in marriage. The evidence accumulated by Hamilton[1] suggests that, among persons of good intelligence, the peak of love affairs for women is at or just before twenty and for men between twenty and twenty-five. There are minor peaks, which probably represent rather flirtations than fully developed love affairs, for girls at fourteen and for boys between fifteen and twenty.

The importance of these preliminary phases of flirtation and trial friendship is that they permit of experiment and allow the world-without-end bargain to be entered on with a vision unclouded by the romantic illusions of early youth. Each should advance a stage further the emancipation of the self from dependence upon the parents, should teach tolerance, and respect for another's personality. Young men and young women who have thought themselves in love many times before are less likely to be bowled over by an overwhelming hunger of the senses and to have their heads turned by the first signs of a reciprocated interest. The danger that flirtation may precipitate into physical expression outside marriage is exaggerated, though recent American research indicates an increase of premarital sex experience

[1] Cited by Hollingworth, loc cit.

among adolescents.[1] Most young people, though less ignorant of the facts of sex than were their parents, have a certain protective fear of physical experience which carries them unscathed through a very close intimacy;[2] and where self-control has been built up on the basis of economics, ethics, and a respect for the rights of another, it is less likely to fail than when founded upon obtrusive parental watchfulness or religious prohibitions. A successful and happy marriage, as Terman's[3] research showed, is dependent more upon the home surroundings of the partners, on the happiness of their childhood, the example of their parents, and on those qualities of personality which have been developed from earliest years, than on such things as sexual compatibility, income, religious training, or virginity at marriage.

Sex Education.[4] If we see healthy sex development as the steady convergence and ultimate integration of two aspects, physical and emotional, of the same psycho-biological source, growing side by side from earliest infancy, we shall be in a position at once to estimate the value or danger inherent in each developmental phase and to decide the broad principles upon which sex education should be based. Knowledge fully and unemotionally imparted to the growing child whenever questions arise, the acceptance by adults of sex as a matter of fact and of course, will do much to prepare for the dramatic physical developments and to prevent the fears and struggles to which ignorance gives rise. Well before puberty the child should be acquainted with the appearance, names, and functions of the organs of both sexes; should know the facts regarding birth and should be in a position to laugh at the stork and gooseberry bush school which confounds innocence with

[1] Partridge, op. cit., pp. 182–3, following Folson, Newcomb, and Bromley
[2] Yates, *Friendships in Adolescence*, p. 9 (London, 1936).
[3] *Psychological Factors in Marital Happiness*, pp. 369 ff.
[4] C. Bibby, *Sex Education* (London, 1944) is a most useful book for parents and teachers. See also the Board of Education pamphlet, No. 119, on the subject H.M.S.O., 1943).

ignorance. Such information comes best from beloved parents, not as something imparted as an awful secret in hushed voices and on special occasions, but as naturally as the child learns about birds and flowers, oil wells, why daddy has to go to the office, and any of the numerous topics on which eager questions are asked. As such, sex education begins with the child's first question and may be put on a comprehensive basis by adequate scientific teaching in school.

Armed in this way with information, the pre-adolescent is less liable to the shock which the unprepared receive when given garbled versions by playmates, or corrupt adults. Such factual education should be complete prior to puberty. It is essential too that the phenomena of menstruation, of nocturnal emission, and of masturbation should be viewed in their true light and divested of exaggerated emotional significance. The girl should be informed of the biological meaning of her monthly periods and taught to rejoice in it as a symbol of her femininity. Some psychic tension before and possibly during the period is normal, but pain and prostration are usually more symptomatic of wrong psychological attitudes than a necessary concomitant of the period. Medical research is rapidly dispersing the superstitions which from time immemorial have surrounded it. In the sex training of the girl, on this topic, it is important to avoid the suggestion that menstruation is an illness, that it is unclean, 'the curse of Eve', or even that it need lead to greatly diminished activity. She should be encouraged, but not forced, to take exercise as at any other time, to bathe, and to mix freely with contemporaries. In the same way, the right attitude should be built up towards childbirth as a thing to be accepted joyously rather than as a fearsome ordeal. Thus many fantasies and much maladjustment of the emotional life will be avoided.

The boy too should be forewarned. He should be reassured on the subject of the effects of masturbation and should be told that while emissions are normal at his age, and even later under

6

special circumstances, self-manipulation, like any other form of self-indulgence, is something which should be kept in bounds. It is necessary energetically to combat the fear of insanity, or of mental or physical deterioration, which is still woefully current and the cause of so many crises in the lives of the young.

It seems advisable too that both sexes should know precisely the facts about venereal disease. Many a youth is haunted by a groundless fear that he has caught something from a towel or public lavatory and passes through untold agonies. One boy tried to purchase a revolver to shoot himself because he thought a discharge of semen a symptom of venereal disease; another worried for weeks over the appearance of hair follicles on his genitals. Public opinion on this subject has advanced in the last few years but there is still much room for misunderstanding in the minds of the young.

Emotional Training. A knowledge of the facts of development is however not enough. One can be well instructed on the anatomy and physiology of sex without having a well adjusted emotional attitude, and it is precisely in this field that right training is most important and most difficult. The sentiment of sex is built throughout life and the child's ideals will be influenced first by the home. The attitudes of the parents to each other, the unconscious emotional complexes governing their acceptance of their own sex role, the genuineness or otherwise of their love for each other, the presence or absence in their manner, of embarrassment over natural functions—all these and a thousand more will reverberate in the minds of their children, and do much to determine their development.

The quickening of the emotional life generally, and of the sex interests in particular, at adolescence offers a great opportunity for emotional training, for the maturing of right attitudes and the eradication of wrong ones. Each one of the emotional experiences of the growing girl or boy—the crush, hero-worship, the passionate friendship, the flirtations, the romantic first love—is educative in the highest degree. Each should be tending towards a truer conception of the personality of another, should bring the self into sharper focus, and should be teaching respect and tolerance, stripped of illusions but pregnant with idealism.

Emotional control and integration on the highest level of which the individual is capable will not however come about unaided. Education for the adolescent should recognize this and seize upon the new social awareness for giving practice in living with others, in accepting responsibility, and in behaviour. At home the adolescent should be encouraged to give and receive hospitality without too much adult participation or supervision. His or her friendships, however mawkish they may seem, should be respected and not be made the subject of witticisms, or worse—of jealous scenes. Unchaperoned expeditions away from home, youth hostelling and the like, days out cycling or walking, the pursuit of common interests, the common sharing of difficulties and inconvenience, of effort and self-denial, are an essential preparation for maturity.

On the school however rests the responsibility for the refinement of emotional response through aesthetic education. If interest in music, the arts, and particularly in literature, is to arise at all, it is most likely to dawn in the late teens. The intensification of a taste for reading can be directed so that, finding his struggles reflected in books, his ideals coherently set forth in action, his philosophy taking shape in eternal verse, the youth loses something of his loneliness and sees himself truly at one with the past and future of his race.

CHAPTER IV

'MOONISH YOUTH'

Evanescence of Adolescent Emotional Experiences. Though the developments in the sex life which we have just been considering are of cardinal importance to a study of our field, the emotional life is evolving in many other ways. Many adults are unable to remember clearly the emotional disturbances of their own adolescence and are disposed to deny that they themselves were anything but calm and collected during the period. Nothing is more evanescent than the memory of emotion, especially if it is attached to experiences which mean something very different at another stage of development; and, for those who have secret diaries kept during their teens, or who come across old letters, essays, pieces of verse, short stories, and the like written during the period, it is an instructive, and probably painful, experience to reread them in the late twenties or thirties. Poets and artists seem able to revive within themselves something of that intense susceptibility to emotion which seems peculiar to some adolescents; and in this awareness of their own past women seem superior to men.

Sources of Information. Information about the emotional life of adolescents is difficult to obtain, since each developing child is apt to consider that his own feelings are different from those of others and to attempt a concealment the more difficult to penetrate in proportion to the intensity of the disturbance. Much therefore of our information is derived from diaries written at the time, from a study of delinquent or neurotic adolescents, from the reports of the more self-conscious and intelligent who continue at school after fourteen, and from the retrospections of adults. Such data may well be sophisticated by the special nature of the groups studied or by the age of the subjects. In order to supplement it by a picture of the more ordinary adolescent in the early teens, the present writer collected reports from 196 boys and girls, all but 41 of whom were between the ages of fourteen and sixteen, and the remainder under the age of eighteen. Rather less than half had left school at fourteen to enter offices and factories and the others were attending full-time technical or commercial courses. The group can therefore be considered representative of adolescents of average ability from lower-middle and working-class homes.[1]

Each answered a questionnaire containing a large number of items. Each was assured of secrecy: no names were put on the papers, which were sealed up on completion. All were asked to cross out any question which they did not wish to answer or to hand in a blank sheet if they were not prepared to be absolutely frank. The fullness of the replies suggests that these young people entered into the spirit of the inquiry and that they did their best to answer as truthfully as they could. Against one source of error inherent in surveys of this kind it was not possible to guard—the tendency to unconscious falsification through the inability to express feelings, through misunderstanding of the questions, or through the operation of unconscious factors. In the present case, such errors might be expected to minimize, rather than exaggerate, the incidence of the changes studied—especially as the questions were framed carefully to avoid any suggestion of what constituted a desirable answer.

Intensification of Instinctive Drives. Some of the results of this inquiry have been mentioned earlier and more will be given in Chapter V. Tables I and II are confined to an analysis of those sections of the questionnaire which deal especially with the

[1] Replies to some sections of this questionnaire have already been alluded to in Chapter II.

emotional life at this stage of development. In Table I are shown the proportions of boys and girls who record intensifications in certain major fields. The actual question asked was: 'In which of the following have you taken more or less interest since you were about thirteen? (Cross out first of all any in which you are not now and never were interested at all.)' There followed twenty-four topics (listed in full in Table III, Chapter V), some of them covering more intellectualized expressions of emotion and interest. Those given here are the ones which might be held referable to the primary innate dispositions, or to the sentiments, or complexes of emotionally toned ideas based directly upon them, and relatively independent of the effects of differing levels of intelligence. Hence each is given in the table under a schematic heading which suggests the main motive force or forces which underlie it—though of course into almost all of them many other things enter. Table II presents the results of a number of other questions which illuminate some of the changes in Table I and bring collateral evidence of the scope and effects of development in these formative years.

TABLE I

QUESTIONNAIRE ON ADOLESCENCE: INTENSIFICATIONS SINCE THE AGE OF THIRTEEN YEARS IN CERTAIN INTERESTS WHICH MAY BE TRACED TO INSTINCTIVE TENDENCIES (196 ADOLESCENTS)

	110 *Girls* per cent.	85 *Boys* per cent.
1 *Sex*—Increased interest in the opposite sex	73.0	70.0
2 *Gregariousness*—Increased interest in social activities	79.0	59.0
3 *Wandering*—Increased interest in expeditions away from home	56.0	56.0
4 *Self-assertion and self-regard*—Increased interest in personal appearance	86.0	66.0
5 *Aggressiveness, assertiveness, and gregariousness*—Increased interest in games and sports	56.0	72.0
6 *Protective and altruistic impulses*—Increased interest in young children and babies	44.0	22.0

TABLE II

QUESTIONNAIRE ON ADOLESCENCE: BEHAVIOUR AND EMOTIONAL
CHANGE

	110 *Girls* per cent. of Group	86 *Boys* per cent. of Group
1 Keeping a regular diary	55·0	29·0
2 *Mood changes*		
(*a*)Fluctuation between being in good spirits one moment to being bored, downcast or fed up the next	70·0	56·0
(*b*) Increased moodiness since thirteen	69·0	46·0
3 *Increased aggressiveness directed at adults*		
(*a*) Finding oneself up against authority		
'Often', and 'Very often'	31·0	34·0
'Not very often', 'Seldom', or 'Never'	69·0	66·0
(*b*) 'Inclined to answer back and do the opposite to what you are told by adults	75·0	66·0
(*c*) More inclined to be rebellious since thirteen	55·0	49·0
(*d*) More inclined to answer back since thirteen	55·0	47·0
4 *Able to confide most secret thoughts to an adult*	73·0	59·0
to friend	30·0	26·0
to parent	28·0	26·0
to brother or sister	11·0	16·0
to relative	13·5	6·0
5 *Attitude to parents*		
Increased love for father	53·0	50·5
Decreased love for father	1·9	3·5
Increased love for mother	67·5	56·5
Decreased love for mother	4·5	5·0
6 *Desire to run away from home*	19·0	38·0
7 *Day-dreaming*		
(*a*) Do not day-dream	2·6	4·5
(*b*) Day-dreaming has *increased* since thirteen	55·0	27·0
(*c*) Day-dreaming has *decreased* since thirteen	16·0	7·0
8 *Night-dreaming*		
(*a*) Do not dream at night	3·0	11·5
(*b*) Night-dreaming has *increased* since thirteen	32·0	17·5
(*c*) Night-dreaming has *decreased* since thirteen	25·0	16·0

From the two tables we obtain a clear view of the intensification in nearly all the major departments of the emotional life both of boys and of girls. Not merely in sex, but in the desire for contact with one's social group, in the urge to assert the self, in the wish to be free of restraint and supervision and to seek new worlds, is this quickening felt. The ferment shows itself too in the most intimate relationships. There is an overflow into the emotional catharsis of confession to a trusted adult or to the dumb pages of a diary. Moodiness, fantasy, and dreaming increase, suggesting that the emotional being is profoundly stirred.

Sex Differences. Clearly discernible too are the early stages of that divergence in development between the sexes which is completed only when the distinctively masculine or feminine cast is assumed by the adult character. Approximately equal percentages of boys and girls report an increased interest in the opposite sex, and in expeditions away from home; nor is there marked difference in the proportions who report increased aggressiveness, and changes in their attitude to their parents. But many more girls than boys report an increased interest in social activities, in their own personal appearance, and in young children and babies. More girls too mention the keeping of a diary, and increased moodiness, day-dreaming, and night-dreaming. More boys than girls note an increased interest in games and sports and in the desire to run away from home.

Bare differences in figures do not, however, give the whole picture. The difference between the sexes is something more than a mere difference of emphasis; it is as much qualitative as quantitative. Something of this has already been shown in the analysis made in Chapter II, of the causes of rebellion mentioned by the boys and girls of this group—the girls chafing at home discipline and the boys being more general in their revolt. It may also be illustrated more fully by the kinds of answer given by girls and boys to other questions in the present questionnaire. Asked to state which person in real life in history, or in fiction, they would most like to be, the boys confined their answers to characters like 'the Prime Minister', 'a successful engineer', heroes of the sporting world, romantic rogues—'the Picaroon, a cracksman', Robin Hood, the 'Saint' —and the more glamorous members of the fighting services— air-gunners, flying officers, Merchant Navy officers, and the like. The ideals mentioned by the girls, on the other hand, are divided between those in which the sexually desirable aspects of womanhood predominate and those which emphasize altruistic or protective impulses. Of the first, 'heroine of a romance book or picture', Betty Grable, Greer Garson, Jeanette Macdonald, and the vague 'film star' may be taken as examples. Of the second, Florence Nightingale, 'a children's nurse', 'mother to a few young children', Edith Cavell, and Grace Darling are illustrative. There are some choices indeed in which aggressive or dominating impulses can be observed. One girl said she would like to be a seaman, two wished to be ringleaders of a gang of schoolgirls, and another chose Amy Johnson.

The subjects of day-dream mentioned by the boys, though there are a few who mention sexually motivated thoughts, are mainly ideas of dominance, their own future success, adventure, 'aeroplanes, ships and other mechanical workings', travel, 'the farm I am going to have and what I am going to do when I get home from school'. In the day-dreams of the girls 'getting married', 'what sort of family I will have', and thoughts of boys apparently bulk large; when their thoughts turn to other things it is to topics like 'stage life', 'entertaining the troops', 'nice clothes', and so on in which display of the person and its social reference are the important features. This difference coheres with that already mentioned in Chapter II between the questions asked by the boys and those asked by the girls. It will be remembered that the boys were mainly preoccupied with questions of scientific fact and current affairs, while the girls were concerned with problems of sex behaviour and social attitudes.

In another question, each was asked to write down the things of which they were most afraid. The differences here, both qualitatively and quantitatively, are striking. All the girls wrote down at least one source of fear, the average number given being two and one-third. Of the boys one-third left the question blank or wrote 'none', and the average number reported by them was one. The most widespread fear among the girls is of darkness, 'dark places at night', 'dark houses', 'dark and lonely roads'—a dread expressed by 42 per cent. of the girls and by only 9 per cent. of the boys. The second category shows an equally pronounced difference. Of the girls 35 per cent. are fearful of rats, mice, spiders, frogs, toads, snakes, and the like, which do not receive a mention by the boys. Fierce animals—bulls, cows, rams, dogs, and horses—are feared by 32 per cent. of the girls but are mentioned by only 12 per cent. of the boys. A quarter of the girls mention such things as drunken men, German prisoners, fierce-looking men, and another 12 per cent. expatiate on more imaginary horrors— murder books or films, ghosts, atrocity stories, haunted houses, churchyards at night, nightmares—the only parallels to which among the boys are the 9 per cent. who express themselves afraid of authority as represented by gamekeepers and policemen and the 14 per cent. whose fears take the abstract form of an interplanetary catastrophe, destruction, ghosts, quicksands, and great heights.

An interesting feature of the fears recorded by both sexes, and one to which we shall return, is the proportion who fear death and illness or violence. Of the girls, 21 per cent. mention death, drowning, suffocation, 'injections and needles', and a further 16 per cent. bombs, air-raids, burglary, accidents, fire, thunder and lightning. Of the boys, while only 9 per cent. mention death and illness, 21 per cent. seem fearful of murder, air-raids, being tortured to death, physical pain, and accidents like a car smash or a collapsing bridge.

In fear arising in personal situations, again, the qualitative difference is marked, though the numbers reporting such fears are about 10 per cent. of each group. The girls fear loneliness, 'saying the wrong things', 'going astray and doing wrong', 'giving people the wrong impression of myself'; the boys, such situations as 'future unemployment', 'not paying my way when I am older', bankruptcy, 'making a bad show of anything', 'doing people bad turns'.

Much the same tendency is observable in the somewhat scanty evidence afforded by this inquiry of the content of the nocturnal dreams of these adolescents. Among those who recorded the main things about which they dreamed, there were many more girls who recorded 'nightmares', 'murders', 'being chased by strange men', and so on: the boys report 'the day's events', and adventure with greater frequency.[1]

From the data provided by this questionnaire, and from other sources, we can piece together the lines of the general emotional development of boys and girls in their teens. We can see too how, from the impact of the environment and increasing self-awareness, as well as from certain innate differences in the balance of the instinctive impulses, the characteristic aspects of masculinity and femininity are finally determined in the adult.

The Boy. Greater aggressiveness both in the affairs of life and in sexual activities is sanctioned and expected in the male by society, even from the early years of childhood. Hence, any innate differences between the sexes in this respect we should expect to find exaggerated by social pressures. The picture we have of development in the early teens in the boys of this group is one of increased aggressiveness tending to seek overflow at first in a general revolt against adults, in sport, and in the quest for

[1] Kimmins, *Children's Dreams*, ch. v (London, 1920) comments on the falling off, after fourteen, in fear dreams among the boys, an increase of the death element in the dreams of girls, an increase in dreams of bravery and adventure among the boys, and, in both sexes, an increase in references to school activities.

more or less impersonal knowledge. In the early years of
adolescence the boy is, not uncommonly, untidy, dirty, irrespon-
sible, assertive, given to fisticuffs and roughness—a hooligan,
in short, who disdains as unworthy and effeminate all attention
to the niceties of civilized living. It is a phase which corresponds
with the peak age for male delinquencies and with a marked
impulse to form gangs which may unite under hair-raising names
to terrorize a neighbourhood.

To such gangs, the opposite sex is frequently as much an
object of the chase as of purely sexual attractiveness. One little
Camorra of my acquaintance prided itself upon the fine collection
of girls' hair-ribbons which it had acquired. Organized games
—the rougher the better, frequently—provide another outlet
for this gregariousness and pugnacity. The writer well remembers one adolescent rugby enthusiast chanting to his approving
comrades:

   ... Oh! let the hours be short,
   Till fields and blows and groans applaud our sport!
and:

   We must have bloody noses and cracked crowns,
   And pass them current too ...

Slightly later in the development of the boy, gregariousness
may become more socialized; attention becomes focused on the
self, but it is a self for many, in which the aggressive dominating
elements are uppermost, as can be seen from the ideals which
boys adopt and from their day-dreams. It would be rash to say
that sexually motivated thoughts are absent. Few boys, indeed,
mention marriage and children, which are a constant theme with
girls, or the idea of service to others; but sexual curiosity is
probably strong quite early with many. In the early teens the
sexuality of the boy, while it may prompt him to a general
(and often carefully concealed) interest in girls, seems to be
predominantly auto-erotic.[1] Self display and showing-off are

[1] See Chapter III.

frequently the first methods of approach, followed by the rough horseplay which accompanies the early flirtations. Early impulses to approach an individual girl, singled out from her fellows, may be inhibited for a long time by the fear of ridicule, and tenderness or devotion is late in developing.

The Girl. The emotional development of the girl, when it is studied in detail, is very different. At adolescence, as many girls as boys in the present survey reported an increased tendency to rebellion against adults; but this aggressiveness is shown in emotional and social contexts very different from those of the boy. Aggressiveness in a girl is not fostered by society to anything like the extent that it is encouraged in a boy. Moreover, it seems to be associated in her development with increases in tender, protective feeling, and in a greater proneness to the inhibiting emotion of fear, in both of which innate sex differences are increased by social pressures.

Hence the assertiveness of the girl tends to take the form of answering back; and experience suggests that, whereas overt aggression is common with the boy, at home, at school, and among his comrades, the girl is more inclined to passive resistance, to sullenness and withdrawal. The writer well remembers one adolescent girl who, rather than carry out the suggestion that she should do some drawing, sat with a drawing-board and paper on her knee for a whole afternoon, smiling when she was addressed but deaf to all urgings. The boys in the group thought her stupid: the other girls, whilst not imitating or appearing to sympathize with her stand, showed a mysterious understanding of her feelings.

So too the gregariousness of the girl seeks a different expression. Gangs of girls are far less common than gangs of boys. The tendency is for girls to form loose societies within which are pairs of close friends wrapped up in each other. The impact of such mixing with others is shown, not so much by the desire to dominate by feats of prowess, but in an increased interest in the self as it strikes others in its more passive aspects—in what is worn, in manners, speech, behaviour—an interest in which ranks as the most compelling of all the interests of the girl at this stage of development (see Table III, Chapter V) and probably, for many women, constitutes the major preoccupation of their lives.

This interest in the social aspects of the self has as a corollary a more intense scrutiny of the inner life which is doubtless fostered by the earlier maturity of the girl sexually and by a predominance in her psychological make-up of those impulses and emotions which react mainly upon the self, turning inwards rather than outwards—like fear, grief, self-submission, and so on. These may be, and frequently are, accompanied by an introspectiveness which finds vent in the writing of diaries and in intimate confidences bestowed on friends and parents. Over half the girls as compared with little more than a quarter of the boys claimed, in the present investigation, to maintain a private diary; nearly three-quarters of the girls, but only rather more than half of the boys, felt the impulse to confide their most secret thoughts to an adult.

The evidence reported in this chapter from young adolescents coheres with that from delinquent and older groups. Burt[1] as a result of his studies of delinquency, comes to the conclusion that the one well-established difference between the sexes is in the relative dominance of two major groups of instinctive impulses. He points out that the crimes committed by boys are those prompted by one or other of the aggressive impulses—anger, assertiveness, curiosity, acquisitiveness, and the like. Hence boys are prone to crimes of violence, excessive fighting, burglary, wandering, and so on. The girl, on the other hand, is more susceptible to the inhibitive impulses—fear, grief, sorrow, disgust, self-submissiveness, and so on. She is therefore generally less prone to delinquency, and the faults she more frequently

[1] *The Young Delinquent*, pp. 491–2, and Table, pp. 15–16.

commits are lying and attempted suicide, which spring from the inward-turning impulses. Sex offences which are also more characteristic of girls tend to reach their maximum in later adolescence when physical maturity has been attained. Hence it follows that while the peak age for the detected delinquencies of boys is thirteen, the greatest number of detected female delinquencies occurs at the ages of eighteen and nineteen.[1]

Olive Wheeler[2] carries the matter a stage further. From her study of groups of students and workers she concludes that, in the male, the impulses which tend to predominate are egotistic —the desire to assert the self, to dominate and to achieve— whereas, in the female it is those which have social reference which are in the ascendant. Such a suggestion is strikingly confirmed both by the analysis which she gives of the day-dreams of her group and the similar tendency noted in the reveries recorded in this chapter from these younger children.

Sources of Conflict. It is into this system of emotionality that the powerful feelings associated with sex—which Burt finds usually falls among the aggressive impulses—have to be inte-grated at adolescence. For the boy the process seems relatively simple. The energy of the sexual impulses reinforces the egotistic aggressive trends. The desire to assert the self may be expressed in the attainment of economic independence which in turn makes marriage possible. The necessity of choice between marriage and a career rarely presents itself. The teens for very many present a simple progress forward to the attain-ment of compatible goals. Friction is incidental but not inevit-able; hence the boy is usually less moody, less inclined to introspection, less subtly aware of the movements of his own mind, less inclined to find recompense in absorbing day-dreams than the girl. To the girl in whom ambition has kindled, the

[1] Carr Saunders, Mannheim, and Rhodes, *Young Offenders,* p. 52, and Appendix, pp. 160–5 (Cambridge, 1942).
[2] *The Adventure of Youth,* pp. 75–6; 'Variations in the Emotional Development of Normal Adolescents, *B. Journ. Ed. P.,* vol. i, pt. 1, 1931.

conflict between sex and a career must soon present itself. In the early stages of adolescence it seems likely that the power of the sex instinct reinforces her weaker aggression; but quite early the more narcissistic and self-regarding elements of her psychological make-up prevail and she becomes more interested in herself as an object of love and admiration, as the quarry and not as the hunter. The conflict may begin quite soon between the social emotions, which turn her thoughts to a home and babies or to ideas of service to others, and her weaker egotistic impulses, which might make her envious of the distinction open to the boy. The genesis of such a conflict is indeed seen clearly in those girls of the present group who choose masculine heroes, or dominating rather than cherishing or sexually desirable women. There is reason to surmise that this conflict is more pronounced in highly intelligent women[1] to whom a professional career is open, and may well explain the fact that, although there is no essential difference in average intellectual ability between the sexes, fewer women than men attain eminence in professional or public life.

Fantasy, Dreams, and Moods. That for many children, and especially for girls, this transformation of the emotional life is not achieved without difficulty is shown by the proportions who report increased fantasy, night-dreaming, and moodiness. Each of these is a way in which the deep-seated drives of the personality, entirely or partially thwarted in the daily life, find an outlet. The emotional tensions of the adolescent and the lack of developed techniques of redirection or sublimation of emotional dispositions inevitably produce frustrations and conflicts which can, temporarily at all events, find no other escape.

Day-dreams, as was pointed out in Chapter II, are a form of play in which the demands of reality are for the time abrogated though perhaps not entirely forgotten. They may perform many functions: it is from day-dreams not too far removed from

[1] See Chapter VII.

possibility that ambition and workable schemes for the future arise; art too is an embodied projection of fantasy. On the other hand they may provide a catharsis, or an indulgent respite from the narrow claims of the real here and now. It is only when the disproportion between desire and cold fact grows too great and the hold on reality slips that danger arises.

Many of the desires which spring from instinctive sources are, however, incompatible in any form with waking fantasy. Jealousies of brothers and sisters, aggressive wishes against the parents, many sex thoughts to which shame has become attached, are thrust into the deepest layers of the mind, inaccessible to consciousness. Such emerge only when conscious control is most deeply in abeyance as it is in sleep. Deepest of all lie emotional complexes so incompatible with the standards of waking life that, if they emerge at all, even in dreams, they are so heavily disguised in symbols that they are hard for analysis to detect; or they fly, even in their dream form, beyond waking recall. The quickening emotional life in adolescence is apt to reanimate or reinforce such deeply repressed desires, wishes, and fears. If they threaten to break through the barrier of repression, the mind reacts with anxiety or fear, which appears causeless since the cause is so deeply hidden. On the other hand an equally (apparently) causeless elation may be the reaction to some unconscious appeal to buried impulses of self-assertion. Such deeply repressed systems may provoke dreams which are forgotten on waking but which determine the mood of the succeeding day, or they may be so well organized as to be almost a co-conscious personality which inspires apparently causeless changes in the feeling tone from hour to hour.[1] The somatic disturbances of adolescence, particularly glandular upset even when it is slight, the heightened susceptibility to the environment, and the difficulties of adjustment which beset the period may·unite to facilitate such disintegrative processes.

[1] McCurdy, *The Psychology of Emotion* (London, 1925).

7

It is not therefore surprising to find large proportions of boys and girls reporting increased moodiness and fluctuations of emotional tone. With some the swings are mild; with others violent. In extreme cases we get the picture of cyclic insanity —of moods of acute melancholia followed by periods of elation, in both of which, all touch with reality is lost. Some boys and girls tend to project their unconsciously determined anxieties and fears (and sometimes their desires) on to the environment, seeking an object on which to discharge their feelings. Such perhaps is one of the explanations of the more or less irrational fears recorded earlier in this chapter—the girl reacting against her sexual urges by a fear of dark places at night, of molestation by German prisoners, or rough-looking men, and the boy projecting his aggressiveness on to natural forces, interplanetary catastrophes, earthquakes and the like, which may direct their aggression against himself.

As adjustment to reality, and control of the emotional life, are gradually achieved, and as more and more legitimate outlets and redirections for the instinctive energies are found, fantasy, dreaming, and moodiness diminish. None of us however finds a completely satisfactory relationship to our environment; hence these three closely related activities continue throughout life, though the themes and the roots from which they spring vary. The high pitch of intensity which is not uncommon in adolescence, would be abnormal in maturity and would indicate some serious maladjustment; our assessment of the possible dangers to future stability in adolescent moodiness, or daydreaming must therefore be based upon a scrutiny of the provoking factors in the emotional life and in the external environment.

Wandering. The general intensification of the emotional life of which we have been speaking so far, may seek many other outlets or give rise to other characteristic moods in the adolescent. A glance at Table I will show that high proportions both of boys and of girls report an increased interest in expeditions away from home. The roots of such a desire are obscure and many motives may combine; but it does not seem unlikely that there is a rudimentary migratory impulse[1] which, with increasing physical power, experience and growing self-reliance, prompts the desire to get away from the familiar environment of home or street. Each week-end in the spring and summer sees pairs and clubs of young people seeking the 'wild wood and the downs'. Expeditions on cycles into the night, rambles in the country, explorations of remoter parts of the city, continuous and unceasing travel on buses, trams and underground railways, daydreams of distant lands, visions of Chimborazo and Cotopaxi—all these in their differing ways are symptoms of the same restless urge to seek fresh woods and pastures new. This 'locomotor restlessness' may ally itself with other impulses asserting themselves vigorously in the teens—with the desire for fierce physical activity which some show, with sex, with an enlivened curiosity, with the impulse to hunt, or with an acquisitive tendency seeking expression in a collection of photographs, fossils, butterflies, birds' eggs, or wild flowers. One sixteen-year-old of my acquaintance went cycling in the long dark evening hours of the early part of the year to find solitude. Two others, pursuing dawning interests in natural science, a newly discovered delight in each other's company and the desire to test the limits of their own physical endurance set themselves the task of covering as much distance and seeking as much knowledge of wild life as they could in four days. They tramped 130 miles and on their return slept for over twenty-four hours. Others, in whom gregarious impulses are pronounced, enjoy the wide companionship of large camps or youth hostels.

Such excursions away from home, far from being hindered by motives of caution, should be encouraged. For, apart from the satisfaction which they give to powerful drives, they are part of the process of psychological weaning from the domination

Burt, op. cit., pp. 456–7.

of the parents. The boy or girl who shows no desire to get away from the home and its cherishing supervision may be seeking to prolong the process of growing up, may be suffering from crippling conflicts or finding maladaptive satisfaction in a surrender to day-dreams.

Wandering or the desire to wander may however be prompted by other and more serious causes. Of Valentine's student group,[1] 40 per cent. of the men and 35 per cent. of the women confessed that they had at one time or another contemplated running away from home. The proportions in the present writer's younger group (Table II) are smaller but similar. The nature of the emotional state which prompts such thought is well revealed in the words of one of my own graduate students, who writes: 'In a moment of extreme anger [with her mother] I thought of leaving home and made plans even to the extent of leaving a bitter farewell note. Practical details such as where I should go, how I should live were not considered. . . .' Two American studies of adolescents who did[2] actually run away from home indicated a heavy preponderance in both sexes (sixty-eight out of seventy-six cases) of those who gave reasons implying a desire to escape from unpleasant situations in the home and especially from conflict with father or mother.

Suicidal Thoughts. Overt conflicts with the environment are probably also the conscious reason for some of the suicidal thoughts of the adolescent, since both running away and self-destruction are not uncommonly thought of as a means of punishing an unsympathetic family or parent. 'They'll be sorry when I'm dead' may lead to fantasies in which the funeral, the flowers, the remorseful friends, relatives, and parents are all pictured. We have seen too how frequent is the thought of

[1] 'Adolescence and Some Problems of Youth Training', *B. Journ. Ed. P.*, vol. xiii, pt. 2, 1943.
[2] Albert, *Some Factors Related to Running Away among Adolescents.* Howe, 'Runaway Girls in New York', *Smith College Studies in Social Work*, vol. ix, No. 2, 1938.

death among the fears, especially of adolescent girls. It seems strange that, just when the capacity for enjoyment seems enhanced, the thought of death should occur, sometimes as a fear that banishes sleep lest the heart should stop beating, sometimes coupled with intense experience, sometimes as an alluring experiment. The suggestion has been made that the pre-occupation with 'worms and epitaphs' is mysteriously connected with rapid growth, and, especially in girls, with fantasies of pregnancy.[1] Flügel[2] argues that where the thought of death leads to the contemplation of, or an actual attempt at, suicide, it is what he calls *nemesism*, the turning upon the self of aggressive impulses not permitted expression against others, usually the parents. Moods of intense dejection such as are reported by more than 60 per cent. of Valentine's students are perhaps obscurely motivated thus though the general threat by invigorated instinctive forces to the barriers of repression built up in childhood may well be the more general cause.

Threats of suicide and the contemplation of it are more common than serious attempts. In Valentine's group,[3] although about a third confessed to having contemplated suicide, only two actual attempts were reported. Among serious attempts, Burt[4] found that excess of grief was rarely a major cause; but the desire to punish others, over-pressure at school, homesickness, and, in the later teens, the pangs of despised love or of jealousy may be potent motives. It is in the late teens too that sporadic cases of *folie à deux* occur, in which two young people prevented by parents or circumstances from marrying, die together. In others, the thought of death becomes fascinating to the extent that experiments with ropes, shotguns, and the like are carried out, sometimes with accidentally fatal results.

Such a fascination too may account for the delight which the

[1] Deutsch, *The Psychology of Women*, vol. i, pp. 175–9.
[2] *Man, Morals and Society*, pp. 81–3 (London, 1945).
[3] loc. cit., p. 58 and n.
[4] op. cit., pp. 485 ff.

young find in the more gloomy and pessimistic verse of our own and foreign literature. One small group of boys in a sixth form for a time adopted De Vigny's *Mort du Loup* as embodying their final philosophy of life—a stoic resignation which could only flower in an early death. We are told too that the publication of *The Sorrows of Werther*, of Artzibashev's *Sanin* and Weininger's *Sex and Character*, was in each case followed by a wave of suicides among adolescents.[1]

Mid-adolescence a Climacteric? In this there seems to be something of a crisis in the middle teens. In her study of the moral conceptions of children, Eve Macaulay[2] finds that suicide is not mentioned as a crime before the age of eleven; and, up to the age of fourteen, by not more than 3 per cent. At the age of fifteen, the proportion of mentions rises abruptly to 23 per cent. and at sixteen to 30 per cent. after which it declines until from nineteen onwards it is mentioned only by 10 per cent. This agrees with the evidence presented by Hall[3] who suggests that the 'curve of despondency' reaches its peak at or just after fifteen.

There are other indications that at some time in the mid-teens there is a climacteric, after which some of the tumult in the emotional life subsides, leaving the way clear for more intellectualized developments in the mental life. After the age of fifteen to sixteen there is a marked decline in the number of male delinquents which suggests that the instinctive life is more fully in control. So too, in her research previously mentioned, Macaulay found that from fifteen to sixteen onwards 'sins of the spirit'—selfishness, hypocrisy, moral and spiritual cowardice —begin to predominate over crimes of violence mentioned by her groups. She states too that, whereas from fourteen to sixteen there is a steadily increasing number of both sexes who, when

[1] Spiel, 'Books in General', *New Statesman and Nation*, February 16th 1946.
[2] Macaulay and Watkins, 'An Investigation into the Development of the Moral Conceptions of Children', *Forum of Ed.*, vol. i, Nos. 1 and 2.
[3] *Adolescence*, vol. i, pp. 374–84; vol. ii, p. 77.

asked whom they would most like to resemble, reply 'I want to be like no one but myself'; this is a choice which disappears after the age of sixteen. Austin,[1] in her study of the vocational ambitions of adolescents, draws attention to the anomalies shown in the replies of her fifteen-year-olds which suggest that at this age they are finding life particularly difficult. The major peak for adolescent religious conversion for boys was found by Starbuck[2] to be about sixteen and for girls a little earlier.

The change in behaviour may be equally marked. The author and his colleagues were struck, in running an experimental Youth College, with the improvement in steadiness of purpose, the diminution in aggressiveness, and the socializing of all the impulses shown by the same boys and girls after sixteen compared with their excitability, lack of control, and crude emotionalism a year or two earlier—an observation confirmed incidentally by a headmaster of a similar school.[3]

We may perhaps connect the change with maturation in intelligence which, for the average youth, reaches its limit of growth at sixteen or thereabouts. Emotional control depends upon an equilibrium between the restraining and directing power of the intelligence and the strength of the instinctive impulses. It is not, apparently, until the intellectual grasp is almost at its maximum that it is adequate to cope with the newly aroused desires of the adolescent, and the affective life can be disciplined to calmer and less extreme expressions. The point of rest and the age at which it is found will depend upon the strength of the emotionality, the capacity of the intelligence, and the outlets and sublimations offered, as well as on the repressions enforced, by the environment.

Varieties in Behaviour. At the risk of repetition, it must be

---

[1] 'An Analysis of the Motives of Adolescents for the Choice of the Teaching Profession', *B. Journ. Ed. P.*, vol. i, pt. 1, 1931, p. 96.
[2] *The Psychology of Religion* (London, 1914).
[3] Fearnley Lane, 'In Praise of the Day Continuation School', *Occ. Psych.*, vol. xvii, No. 2, 1943.

re-emphasized that wide generalizations about the emotional developments of adolescence are difficult and probably valueless if they are applied unmodified to individual boys and girls. As the evidence cited in this chapter suggests, there is a great range of variation both in the age at which developments take place, in the intensity of the emotions felt, and even whether certain developments occur at all. Some of this variation is a matter of individual constitution; some of it due to differing experiences and environmental stimulus; some of it, as we shall see in the next chapter, springs from difference in intellectual level. One thing however does seem to be certain : For most, the early teens for a variety of reasons are a period of insecurity greater than is normally to be expected at any other stage in life.

It is this uncertainty both about the control of powerful feelings and over the way in which the new demands of life are to be met which accounts for the instability of adolescent behaviour. Conduct at one time may show curious regressions to patterns discarded in childhood and at others an unexpected maturity; abnormal aggressiveness, morose depressed withdrawal, arrogant self-assertion, elation, conceit, bumptiousness —in fact all those extremes of behaviour that indicate a spirit in ferment—may be expected as a part of development, without anticipating an enduringly serious disturbance. Such manifestations should be treated as signs that adjustment is proving difficult; and steps should be taken accordingly to reduce the strains and pressures to which the personality is reacting.

The trained observer, watching any group of young people will perceive evidence of such upsets. In one group which came under the attention of the writer, more than a quarter showed varieties of behaviour and conduct sufficiently extreme to be described (at any other period of life) as neurotic. Among the boys for example there was a general physical restlessness; in some, this broke out into acts of apparently senseless violence against chairs or tables; in others in noisy, excitable roughness and 'monkey shines'. One boy was given to attracting attention by elaborate 'fits' in which he lay inert upon the floor or apparently lost the use of a limb. Another was obstinately sullen and monosyllabic even with his fellows; another so shy that he blushed whenever he was spoken to; in yet another the passing maladjustment took the form of an officious assigning to himself of hard physical jobs which he abandoned before they were completed. Among the girls, there were as many showing behaviour difficulties. One was found in a small storeroom with the door locked, weeping bitterly because her particular friend had—only temporarily—joined forces with someone else. Another, who always slept between her parents and refused to go to sleep anywhere else, was dominated by strange superstitions and horrified the other girls by stories of attacks upon her by rats. A third did her best, by calculated impertinence alternating with sullen obstinacy or fierce and stormy outbreaks of temper, to occupy the centre of attention. Another delighted some and shocked others of her companions by tales of nocturnal adventures with soldiers—most of which were grossly exaggerated—and by salacious remarks and snatches of song which she intended adults to overhear. A fifth was so inordinately sensitive to the opinion of adults that her eyes filled with tears at the least breath of censure.

Instances of this kind could be multiplied from any group of boys and girls in their early teens. The problem arises as to what a responsible adult, teacher, or youth leader can do to ease the difficulties and upsets of such young people. Undoubtedly there are some in whom the disturbances are so profound that the skilled attention of a psychologist is essential either as a preventive or as a therapeutic measure. Most however can be helped to deal with their conflicts by a knowledge of the causes, and by a manipulation of the environment so that it provides the needed outlet for emotion or a necessary framework of security whilst the crisis lasts.

In the last forty years there has been much research into the emotional development of children.[1] From this it has emerged that defective or uncertain home discipline, parental dissension, lack of affection, over-great attachment to one or other parent, doubt over parentage, unusually harsh treatment, marked physical, social, or economic difference from companions—anything, in fact, which emphasizes difference or contributes to a feeling of insecurity—are peculiarly liable to cause emotional difficulties in children. Where such conditions exist, they are likely to have their maximum effect at adolescence when they combine with other, less controllable, sources of difficulty to issue in delinquency, psychosis, or more or less serious psychoneurotic disturbance. Hence it follows that amelioration of such conditions at the earliest stage will do much to forestall trouble later. As a positive measure we may emphasize here what is perhaps the cardinal need of the adolescent boy or girl—the need for the secure affection of a trusted adult and for acceptance by contemporaries. 'Whatever you do, we like you; we are willing and anxious to understand your point of view, to give you the chance to achieve independence, to meet you on an equal footing, and to give you your share of attention. We prefer that you should act thus and thus; the result will be for the advantage of all of us; but whatever you choose to do, you are sure of our affection'—such an attitude, not of course expressed in so many words, but clearly manifest in the adults in the environment, will do much to diminish the anxieties and fears and conflicts of the growing youth until the techniques have been acquired which will protect the sensitive spirit from the casual blows of social life.

[1] The important subject of the causation of problem and delinquent behaviour in children has been the subject of many investigations and nothing like a complete bibliography can be given here. The classic study in the field is that of Burt (*The Young Delinquent*) to which copious reference has been made. The following will also be found of interest: Healy, *Mental Conflicts and Misconduct* (Boston, 1923); Norwood East, *The Adolescent Criminal* (London, 1942); Ackerson, *Children's Behaviour Problems* (Chicago, 1942); Williams, *The causes of Social Maladjustment in Children*, Univ. of Iowa Studies in Child Psych., No. xv, 1932.

CHAPTER V

THE MIND GROWS UP

I. INTELLIGENCE AND SPECIFIC ABILITIES

General Intelligence. Although we have so far concentrated upon the emotional developments of adolescence, we should not fall into the error of underrating the intellectual aspects of the mind. The emotions provide the springs of action, but the intellect adapts their crude energy to the business of social living. The desirable result of growing up would be a personality in which the emotions are under the control of the intelligence and in which the intelligence provides for the emotional energies outlets which are not merely satisfactory to the individual but of service to the community.

Intelligence has been defined by Burt as 'inborn, general, intellectual efficiency',[1] and by Victoria Hazlitt as 'the problem solving organization of mind'.[2] Spearman, on the basis of his own and others' researches, describes it as the ability to perceive the essential relationships between items of knowledge and to make use of those relationships to educe further correlative thoughts apposite to the matter in hand. For example, if we perceive the essential relation between 'hat' and 'head', it can be applied to find a word to complete the relation 'glove ———?' Spearman demonstrated mathematically that this ability enters in greater or lesser degree into all conscious activities and, to avoid the inaccuracies and misconceptions surrounding the word intelligence, he called it 'g'.[3]

[1] *The Subnormal Mind*, p. 23 (Oxford, 1937).
[2] *Ability*, p. 24 (London, 1926).
[3] *The Nature of Intelligence and the Principles of Cognition* (London, 1923).

Innateness of Intelligence. It is also generally agreed that this general factor 'g' is innately determined[1] a property of the nervous organization, which, although disease may stunt its growth, is not a product of education, experience, knowledge, or environmental influences. Throughout the first two decades of life there is an increase or maturation in this general ability which roughly keeps pace with physical age. During the few years after birth growth is very rapid until, at age four, about a third of the maximum for the individual is reached. The rate of maturation seems to slow down somewhat after that, but by the age of eleven about four-fifths of maximum capacity is attained. Thereafter the increments are much smaller; until, for all except the supernormal, growth in inborn capacity ceases in the mid-teens at about sixteen.[2]

Intelligence Quotient. For practical purposes it is possible by a knowledge of the average capacity of children at various stages of chronological development, to establish a mental age scale. Such, in fact, is the basis of the well-known *Binet Tests* and the many tests founded upon them. These contain a series of graded problems of increasing difficulty, all of them designed to evoke intelligent behaviour and assigned to the level at which 75 per cent. of children of that chronological age last birthday are able to solve them.[3] Thus if a child can solve all the problems appropriate to his chronological age, his mental level is average for his years; if he solves those of an age level higher

[1] A concise summary of the evidence in favour of the innateness of 'g' is given by Burt in his article 'Ability and Income', *B. Journ. Ed. P.*, vol. xiii, pt. 2, 1943; and the whole topic of intelligence testing is dealt with by Knight in his book *Intelligence and Intelligence Testing* (London, 1933).

[2] C. A. Richardson and C. W. Stokes, *The Growth and Variability of Intelligence, B. Journ. P.* Monog. Suppt. No. 18, p. 30. See also Dearborn and Rothney, *Predicting the Child's Development*; Jones and Hsai, 'Differences in Mental Growth and Decline', *Journ. Ed. Psych.*, vol. xxiv, No. 3, 1933.

[3] Burt, *Mental and Scholastic Tests* (London, 1921). The method of measuring development by means of the Intelligence Quotient or Mental Age from which it is derived has much against it from the mathematical and scientific viewpoints. It is however the method most generally in use, and is effective for rough comparative and diagnostic purposes.

than his own, he is advanced; and if he is able to solve only those problems appropriate to a child younger than himself he is retarded in intellectual development. The relationship between a child's mental age and his chronological age is frequently represented by a percentage ratio—the *Intelligence Quotient* or *I.Q.* arrived at by the formula:

$$\frac{\text{mental age}}{\text{chronological age}} \times 100$$

Thus a mental ratio of 100 is average, of more than 100 above average, and below 100 subaverage.

Common sense confirms what research has shown, that there are wide variations in ability among children and adults. All men, at least in intellectual capacity, are not born equal. In fact, it seems that inborn intelligence is distributed in the population in a way very similar to height or many other biological characteristics—that is, there are a great many who fall round about the average and a much smaller number who are of a very high or very low capacity. Plotted as a curve, the frequencies with which the various intelligence quotients of an unselected sample of schoolchildren of a given chronological age occur would produce a bell-shape familiar to statisticians as the 'curve of error'. Roughly three-quarters would have intelligence quotients falling around the average of 100 I.Q. and between the limits of I.Q. 85 and I.Q. 115; while below I.Q. 85 would be found rather more than 12 per cent.[1] and above 115 rather less than 12 per cent. of the group.

It has been found too that the supernormal mature intellectually at a greater than average rate and the subnormal at a slower than average rate. This differential speed of development means that, as time goes on, the differences in ability, apparent in early childhood, increase: but these different rates are such that, although there are a few exceptions, the

[1] The lower end of the curve is swollen by the small proportion whose intelligence has been affected by birth injury, cretinism, and other pathological factors.

intelligence quotient itself remains approximately constant.[1] The effect of this is best illustrated by an example. A child who on his fifth birthday has an I.Q. of 115—i.e. 15 per cent. higher than average—will have a *mental* age equal to that of the average child of 5 years 9 months. A child of the same chronological age but with an I.Q. of 85 will have a *mental* age of 4 years 3 months. Between these two children there is thus a difference equivalent to 1½ years of mental growth. Ten years later when both reach the chronological age of fifteen, the brighter child will have a *mental* age of 17 years 3 months, and the duller of 12 years 9 months—a difference of 4½ years of mental growth. If we take a greater extreme and consider the difference at adolescence and later, between very high ability (say I.Q. 150 and above) and the borderline of mental defect (I.Q. 70), the range is even more striking and may be 12 mental years or more.

The Effects of Intelligence on Adjustment. These facts have an important bearing upon our subject. They serve to emphasize from another aspect the wide range of individual variation which will be found in any group of adolescents and the very differing levels on which their mental adjustments to life will be made. There is little or no correlation between mental and emotional development as such; but, in a thousand ways, intelligence modifies behaviour and influences environmental adjustment from birth. Much conduct, for example, depends upon the ability to learn desirable responses, and many moral judgements are dependent upon a thorough understanding of all the

[1] There are some cases of variation in I.Q. which cannot be explained except on the assumption of individual anomalies of growth (vide, for example, Terman, *Genetic Studies of Genius*, vol. iii, pp. 25ff., and Dearborn and Rothney, *Predicting the Child's Development*, pp. 230–7) and some conflicting evidence that there are sex differences in the rate of maturation. In the main, however, marked variations in I.Q. from age to age are ascribable to factors (emotional disturbances, lack of comparable testing material, specific environmental influences, and the like) which are referable rather to weakness in the measure of intelligence than to any marked divergence from a reasonably predictable pattern of growth. Certain diseases like epilepsy may bring about progressive deterioration in the intelligence; and glandular disturbance may have an effect, though the evidence is conflicting on this point.

factors in a given situation. Intelligent appraisal of a situation is frequently necessary before adequate steps can be taken either to achieve a desired result or to compensate for failure or disappointment. The turning aside of the energies of an instinctive drive into channels satisfactory to the individual and acceptable to the community—sublimation as it is called—willl be accomplished very differently at different intellectual levels. Intelligence is in fact the moderator; happy adjustment will depend very largely upon the balance between intelligent control and the power of the emotionality.

The very dull—the mentally defective as they are commonly called—those whose intelligence quotient falls below 70, form a small proportion of our population (about 1-2 per cent.). They are now usually detected and made the subject of special educational provision for the educationally subnormal. It is the child whose intelligence is above this level but below the level for which normal teaching methods and syllabuses are designed and whose low ability renders some degree of educational backwardness inevitable who may feel continued frustration, difficulty, and lack of success in his schoolwork. It is not therefore surprising to find that three-quarters of delinquents are drawn, not principally from the mentally defective, but from the I.Q. range 70-95[1]; nor is it strange to find among those whose progress in school has been markedly poor a high proportion who show emotional disturbance in adult life.[2]

The increased emotional tension of adolescence puts a greater strain on the adaptive power of the intelligence. An adequate sentiment of the self, the acquisition of moral sentiments and their expression in conduct, the processes of integration and of control will all to a large extent depend upon intelligent discrimination.[3] The fourteen-year-old with a mental age of less

[1] Burt, *The Young Delinquent*, pp. 294 ff.
[2] Wall, 'Reading Backwardness among Army Men', pts. i and ii, *B. Journ. Ed. P.*, vol. xv, pt. 1, 1945; vol. xvi, pt. 3, 1946.
[3] Gordon, 'The Problem of Social Adjustment', *Journ. Neur. and Psychopath.*, vol. xliii, 1931.

than twelve is more likely to find the new power of sexual appetites or of increased aggressiveness difficult to cope with satisfactorily than is his more intelligent contemporary.

Vocationally too this lower than average level of ability must operate as a handicap. It has been found that where a job makes demands upon an individual which are beyond his mental powers, anxiety, revolt, excessive day-dreaming, or other symptoms may arise. An adolescent's conception of what will be demanded by his future job may be wildly inaccurate; he may simply view it as an escape from school where his limited ability has been a source of continual frustration; but unless wise guidance or rare good fortune directs him to something within his compass, discouragement, occupational drifting, and unemployment may continue so long as to render him unemployable. Such consequences seem to be peculiarly characteristic of those whose failure to adapt to school was so marked as to lead them to truancy.[1]

The possession of superior intelligence may also have its difficulties, particularly if it is not recognized by the school. Most children with an I.Q. of 115 or higher have in the past been sent to some form of secondary school, grammar or technical, at the age of eleven or a little later. In these more exacting surroundings their adjustment will depend upon how far they diverge from the general level of the more intelligent group in which they find themselves. If they are well below the general average (and cannot therefore fulfil the demands made upon them by parents or teachers) they may become anxious, aggressive or delinquent. Every teacher in a grammar school has experience of boys or girls who adapt badly to the academic curriculum and whose behaviour, especially between the ages of thirteen and sixteen, is very difficult.[2] Not so easily

[1] Lummis, 'The Relation of School Attendance to Employment Records, etc.', *B. Journ. Ed. P.*, vol. xvi, pt. 1, 1946.
[2] See the summary of researches on this point given by C. W. Valentine and W. G. Emmett, *The Reliability of Examinations*, part ii (London, 1932).

identified are those adolescents who, finding the work beyond their capacity, react by quiescence masquerading as laziness or by absorbed reverie.

With the child of outstanding brilliance, the danger arises more from a lack of synchronization between intellectual, emotional, and physical development. A bright boy or girl of thirteen may be physically and physiologically early in puberty and emotionally only on the level of a chronological contemporary; but high intelligence may have accelerated school progress so far that form companions are two or even three years in advance in physical and social development. Such a disparity may well produce in the adolescent quite unwarranted feelings of difference and inferiority—especially in boys' schools, in which physical prowess is the surest way to the esteem of contemporaries.

In general, it seems, difficulty is liable to arise whenever the individual differs markedly in intelligence from the rest of his group or when there are wide discrepancies between the three main fields of development—mental, physical, and emotional. Such disparities can, of course, arise at almost any age, but they are more frequent and more likely to cause trouble at adolescence because individual differences are reaching their maximum and because the increasing awareness of change focuses attention on the self.

Special Abilities. The teens bring other developments in the cognitive field in addition to the slow maturing of general intelligence. Modern research indicates that there are abilities which are, to some extent, independent of general, all-round capacity. Most of us are acquainted with extreme types; for example we are familiar with the kind of man or woman whose thoughts flow easily into words, and the contrasting individual who, although just as intelligent, finds verbal expression difficult. Similarly there are those who are 'hopeless at figures' and others to whom numerical symbols are an easy instrument

8

of thought. Success in any task, it appears, depends upon the general or 'g' factor plus one or more of these 'group' factors, as they are called because they enter into one group of related activities and not into another. Among the group abilities so far identified by experiment are (i) *verbal ability* (v), which seems to consist of two sub-abilities, verbal-literary and verbal-linguistic; (ii) *number* or *arithmetic ability* (n), which enters into all operations involving the manipulation of numerical symbols; (iii) *spatial perception* (k), which is involved in making comparative judgements of areas and shapes, for example in dressmaking; (iv) *manual dexterity*, which seems to be required by most operations requiring skilled use of the hands; (v) *mechanical aptitude* (m), called forth by the understanding and construction of mechanisms, and (vi) *musical* and *artistic* ability.[1] It seems probable that there are other group abilities or 'factors of the mind', not all of them purely cognitive, and that into any task there enters also some factor or factors specific to it.

The degree in which any or all of these group abilities are possessed by an individual and the rate at which they mature shows wide variation. Most of them only become of importance, relative to general ability, in the teens. It is true that a few very exceptional children show marked talent in a specific direction in childhood and this is particularly the case with musical ability; most usually, however, such precocity is as much an expression of high general intelligence as of special gifts. With the majority of children, it seems that at the age of eight to nine, general intelligence is over seven times as important in school progress as verbal ability, seventeen times as important as arithmetical ability, and over twenty times as important as manual ability. Two years later, on the threshold

[1] A mass of research and discussion has developed round the important topic of group abilities. The reader is referred to such books as: Alexander, *Intelligence, Concrete and Abstract*, B. Journ. P. Monograph Suppt. No. 19; Burt, *The Factors of the Mind* (London, 1940); Holzinger, 'Preliminary Report on the Spearman-Holzinger Unitary Traits Study', Reports Nos. 1 and 2, *Psychometrica*, ii, 1935; Thurstone, *Primary Mental Abilities* (Chicago, 1939).

of puberty, the group abilities are becoming more important, but general intelligence is still nearly four times as important as verbal ability, twelve times as important as arithmetical, and six times as important as manual ability. In early puberty, twelve to thirteen, the special abilities are more prominent, but general intelligence is still nearly three times as important as verbal ability, twice as important as arithmetical ability, and four and a half times as important as manual ability.[1] During middle and late adolescence, the evidence suggests that it may be possible to distinguish mental types of a complex kind made up of constellations of capacities and emotionally toned dispositions. Vernon,[2] for example, identified *scientific-mathematical, arts or humanistic,* and *practical* types of ability among his university students, and traces of a literary-scientific division are reported by Shakespeare in his study of elementary-school children.[3]

Such abilities, and the comparative lateness with which they declare themselves, are obviously of great educational and vocational importance. It seems to suggest that eleven is too young an age at which to select children for education supposedly adapted to special abilities, since by that age such abilities are hardly likely to have made themselves felt with certainty. In individual cases, too, the possession of a high or low degree of an important ability declaring itself in the teens may make difficulties. One may, for example, find a boy of considerable general ability who, because his verbal aptitude is low, meets with marked difficulty in the later stages of a grammar-school career; or a girl with a flair for literary subjects who finds mathematics intolerable. It sometimes happens that a special capacity is possessed in a marked degree without commensurate intelligence. Extreme cases of this are rare—the *idiots savants,*

[1] Burt, 'The Education of the Young Adolescent, etc.', *B. Journ. Ed. P.,* vol. xiii, pt. 3, 1943.
[2] 'The Educational Abilities of Training College Students', *B. Journ. Ed. P.,* vol. ix, pt. 3, 1939.
[3] 'An Enquiry into the Relative Popularity of School Subjects in Elementary Schools', *B. Journ. Ed. P.,* vol. iv, pt. 2, 1936, esp. p. 152.

spectacular calculators or musicians who are otherwise mentally defective—but it is not so uncommon to find marked executive ability in say art or music in company with an intelligence no better than average. Where such an anomaly of capacity arises, frustration is not unlikely, especially in the vocational field. In a few cases, one or other of the special abilities of educational importance may be so markedly poor as to produce, for example, a specific retardation in an important field—reading, spelling, or arithmetic—at an early stage in the educational career.[1] Such defects, if not quickly detected and met by special teaching methods, soon become centres of emotional disturbance.

Interests. The cases which we have been citing so far are the exceptions; for most, adolescence brings a maturation, both of the intelligence and of the special capacities, which runs side by side with growth in the emotional and physical spheres. The total effect of development is to bring about a great expansion and differentiation in the field of interests, a complex resultant which cannot be ascribed to growth in one direction only, though the increments in intellectual power, absolutely small in themselves, are fundamental in determining the level at which the interests and capacities of the adolescent will function.

It seems that with about half or more of a normal group of children, intelligence develops in the teens to the stage at which there is a pronounced, even apparently sudden, increase in the ability to reason with the aid of symbols and in the understanding of abstract concepts. For example, at a mental age of six a typical child defines words like 'horse' or 'mother' only in terms of use—'a horse runs or draws a cart', 'she minds the babies'; at a mental age of ten the child will assign the object to its class or describe it: 'an animal', 'one who cooks our dinners', 'a lady'. It is not until a mental age of fourteen that

---

[1] Burt, 'The Relations of Educational Abilities', *B. Journ. Ed. P.*, vol. ix, pt. 1, 1939, p. 47 note.

words like 'kindness', 'justice', or 'charity', can be defined, and not until fifteen, that the average child can give the difference satisfactorily between such concepts as 'pleasure' and 'happiness', 'poverty' and 'misery', 'evolution' and 'revolution'.[1] Cole[2] cites researches which show that from eleven onwards there are steady increases in the capacity to understand allegories, parables, cartoons, and double meanings generally. So too an increasing mastery of educational techniques, wider experience, and growing knowledge cause reasoning to be more used as an instrument of thought, though the absolute changes in power may be small. By fifteen, the adolescent of normal mental calibre or better—though he will have far to go—is equipped emotionally and intellectually to lay the groundwork of a more or less coherent integration of emotional dispositions, interests, spiritual values, and experience on which to frame a mature personality.

II. INTERESTS AND THE FORMATION OF CHARACTER

Some of the raw materials from which such a philosophy will be framed we have already discussed in Chapter IV. The two tables which follow carry the matter a stage further. Table III is based upon the answers of the 196 adolescents described in Chapter IV to a question which asked them to record increases or decreases in interest in a number of fields of activity since the age of thirteen. It gives a picture of the development in boys and girls of normal intellectual calibre in the early and middle teens. Table IV is a composite presentation of data provided by Valentine[3] and Wheeler[4] derived from older groups of probably superior general ability. Between them they show something of the range and development of adolescent interests.

[1] All these examples are taken from Burt, *London Revision of the Binet Scale*.
[2] *The Psychology of Adolescence*, pp. 215–18, cf. Watts, *The Language and Mental Development of Children* (London, 1941), passim.
[3] *Adolescence and Some Problems of Youth Training*.
[4] *The Adventure of Youth*, pp. 56, 73–4.

TABLE III

Proportions of Adolescents of Average Intelligence Reporting Increases in Interest in Various Fields since the Age
of Thirteen (196 Adolescent Boys and Girls aged Fourteen
to Seventeen)

	Per cent. Boys	Per cent. Girls
1 Nature (wild flowers, scenery, gardening, animals, science, biology, astronomy, etc.)	45·4	40·0
2 The lives of great men and women	10·5	14·5
3 Your own personal appearance (dress, hair, figure, face, carriage, etc.)	66·4	86·4
4 The impression which you make on others by:		
(a) Your personal appearance	50·0	60·0
(b) The things you can do	40·7	53·6
(c) The way in which you speak	39·6	53·6
(d) Your manners and behaviour	54·6	60·9
5 Going for expeditions away from your parents	56·0	56·4
6 Sports, physical training, swimming, athletics, etc.	72·0	56·4
7 Making things	42·0	42·7
8 Religion	34·0	38·2
9 Things which older people do or say	32·6	43·6
10 Members of the opposite sex	70·0	72·7
11 Social activities, dancing, clubs, parties, societies, gangs, etc.	59·4	79·0
12 History (historical customs, personages, old buildings, furniture, social life)	21·0	28·2
13 Poetry (of any kind—in books, newspapers, etc.)	9·3	22·6
14 Collecting things—photographs, letters, stamps, autographs	30·1	54·5
15 What your own future is to be	60·5	62·7
16 Books and reading	51·2	69·1
17 Music	32·6	71·8
18 Politics and how the world is governed	39·6	26·4
19 Travelling abroad	43·0	61·8
20 Younger children and babies	22·1	43·6
21 Things to eat and drink	38·4	39·0

TABLE IV

PROPORTIONS OF VALENTINE'S STUDENT GROUPS AND WHEELER'S
STUDENT AND WORKER GROUPS REPORTING INCREASED INTEREST IN
VARIOUS INTELLECTUAL FIELDS IN ADOLESCENCE

	Valentine Students		Wheeler Students		Workers	
	Men	Women	Men	Women	Men	Women
	Per cent.	Per cent.	Per cent.	Per cent.	Per cent.	Per cent.
Nature	61	66	52	57	80	62
Music	69	71	52	66	40	40
Art	54	62	36	49	60	20
Poetry[1]	56	57	55	71	40	18
Religion	78	74	62	61	18	82
Games[2]	73	70	34		11	
Reading	90	79	64		59	

The most marked feature of these tables is the way in which
each records an intensification of interests in almost all the
major fields—an intensification which, to judge by Table III,
is shown in the early teens by more girls than boys. In their
several ways these tables show how adolescence with its maturing of the intellectual and quickening of the emotional powers
opens the mind to a world of new experience.

Confirmatory evidence is supplied by Lancaster's analysis of
200 biographies.[3] Of these, 120 showed a craze for reading at
adolescence; 109 became great lovers of nature; 58 wrote
poetry; 58 showed a great and sudden development of energy;
55 showed great eagerness for school; 53 devoted themselves
for a season to art or music; 53 became very religious; 46 developed scientific interests; 31 were passionately altruistic; 23 became idealists; 15 would reform society. Rothney making a

[1] In Valentine's groups specified as the 'writing of poems', in Wheeler's only
as increased interest in poetry.
[2] In Wheeler's groups reported as a favourite occupation or subject of study
and no separate figures presented for the sexes.
[3] Cited by Hall, Youth, p. 147.

study of American adolescent boys[1] found that vigorous sports, group games, etc., are liked by more than 90 per cent.; between 70 and 80 per cent. enjoy adventure films, reading magazines like *Life* and *Punch*, telling and listening to jokes, reading scientific magazines, visiting museums, going to plays and musical comedies, listening to murder and mystery stories; between 60 and 70 per cent. enjoy reading books on sport, playing cards, reading news summary magazines, arguing about many problems, reading mystery and adventure stories; rather more than half like keeping live pets, arguing about politics, reading about local and foreign political situations, general science, reading book reviews; between 40 and 50 per cent. like dreaming and musing about the problems of life, reading books and articles about people, psychology, modern and classical novels, making collections of stamps, minerals, etc., and debating; rather more than one-third enjoy reading biographies, historical novels, reading poetry, and going to Sunday School; a quarter or less like reading Shakespeare, histories of literature, religious books and papers, philosophic essays, writing poetry, or composing music.

Physical Activity. In this material and that of Tables I and II it is possible to discern a number of tendencies which, although they may express themselves in different forms, appear to be characteristic of the development of adolescent interests. Marked in all groups is the great increase in the delight taken in physical activity, in exertion for its own sake—an expression of exuberance which affects no small proportion of girls as well as boys, and is as much if not more a characteristic of intellectuals as it is of the more nearly average in ability. We have already discussed this as an aspect of the intensification of aggressive and gregarious impulses which may find an outlet in team games. The opportunity which it offers for physical education and for

[1] 'The Interests of Public Schoolboys, *Journ. Ed. Pysch*, vol. xxviii, No. 8, November 1937.

social training, for the disciplining of pugnacity and assertiveness to the needs of the group, for the perfection of muscular
co-ordinations, and for the sheer 'letting off of steam', is one
which we neglect at our peril in education. Yet it should not
be thought that every adolescent boy or girl, all the time,
needs exhausting physical exercise, compulsory games, the
heartbreaking strain of competition with physical superiors.
There is a complementary need for rest, for periods of physical
idling, even for lounging in sheer creature comfort while the
spent energies recuperate.

Reading. A similar burst of energy in the intellectual sphere
is shown by many who develop a craze for reading or for
academic study. Much of this fervid absorption in the printed
word must be ascribed to the food which adventure stories,
novels, and romance provide for a quickening fantasy life; to
some, reading is part of an omnivorous passion for knowledge,
either in a particular field or as a foretaste of what the world
has to offer; others seek in literature some crystallization of their
own vaguely conceived ideals; to yet others, books for the first
time become consciously used as tools in the service of a widening intellectual grasp.

In this field sex differences, and differences between those of
high and of low intelligence, are marked. Throughout adolescence, girls on the average read from 10 to 30 per cent. more
than boys,[1] a difference which continues into maturity,[2] though
among intellectuals and in certain spheres of interest, gifted
boys may equal or surpass girls of the same mental calibre.[3]
In the kind of books read, especially in early adolescence, the
differences are even more pronounced, and show more clearly
perhaps than anything else the differences in the strength of the

[1] Jenkinson, *What do Boys and Girls Read?*, p. 172 (London, 1940). See also
Jordan, *Children's Reading Interests* (Oxford, 1926); Terman and Lima, *Children's
Reading* (New York, 1931); Gray and Munroe, *The Reading Interests and Habits
of Adults* (New York, 1929).
[2] Gray and Munroe, op. cit., pp. 21–3.
[3] See Table IV.

various instinctive forces in the two sexes. These differences begin to become evident at about the age of nine when the boy turns to books of a more realistic nature from the fairy stories which continue to delight the girl.[1] In the early teens the divergence grows wider. The interests of girls are principally concerned with fiction which portrays home life, home and school, and love. 'Those authors popular with girls appeal largely to the following instincts: maternal, kindliness, attention to others, response to approval and scornful behaviour.'[2] With boys, books concerned with war and scouting, school and sports, and strenuous adventure, which appeal to 'instincts of mastery, fighting and love of sensory life for its own sake',[2] are the most popular. It is only in the later teens that boys begin to develop an interest in romantic fiction and even then by no means universally; but increasing numbers of informational books—on hobbies, science, and even current affairs—enter into the choices of the more intelligent.

All the researches which have been made into adolescent reading tastes tend to the conclusion that by the age of fifteen or sixteen generalizations, such as could have been made in the years of childhood, are no longer possible; and much the same range and variety of interests is apparent in an adolescent group as among adults. Intellectual differences are shown in the numbers of books, magazines, and newspapers[3] read, and in the quality of the choices made. Whereas those whose intelligence is not of a high level tend to confine their reading to the poorer sort of trash,[4] the brilliant boy or girl is more versatile in interest and, especially the boy, includes a far greater proportion and range of non-fiction. As one highly intelligent girl puts it, 'At the age of fifteen, I was not a more omnivorous reader than I was previously, but the books I read were of higher standard.

[1] Terman and Lima, op. cit., p. 68.   [2] Jordan, op. cit., pp. 27–8.
[3] For differences in newspaper reading according to age, sex and education see the present writer's paper on 'The Newspaper Reading Interests of Adolescents and Adults', *B. Journ. Ed. P.*, vol. xviii, pts. 1, 2.
[4] Morgan, *Young Citizen*, p. 85 (Penguin, 1943); Green, 'The Teaching of English', II, *Journ. Ex. Ped.*, vol. ii, 1918.

. . . The Rubáiyát of Omár Khayyam gave me such pleasure that I learnt much of it by heart. Browning, Wordsworth, Tennyson, gave me great enjoyment.'

At the other extreme are found those who may perhaps acquire more or less laboriously the techniques of 'barking at print' sufficiently to scrape through school in a state of passive indifference or dislike. When school is left with a sigh of relief, this distaste, reinforced by the disturbances of the early teens and perhaps by the attitude of a social group, results in the lapse of large numbers of boys and girls into semi- or even total illiteracy.[1]

The Cinema. With such youths and even with adolescents of a more normal level of attainment, the cinema must be considered as a mental influence equally potent with the printed word. From the research of the Cinema Commission of Enquiry, it seems that film memories are apt to be more particular and less general than, for example, the memories left by the words of a teacher, and that this particularity remains characteristic of them over a period of at least twelve months.[2] This suggests that film experiences are more vivid and striking than would be for example a verbal description of similar happenings—a matter of some importance when we consider the content of films in relation to adolescent inexperience. Even in this respect, however, frequency of attendance may tend to blur the sharpness of memory; and increasing age seems to bring an increasingly critical approach, especially in the more intelligent, to the 'realities' of the screen.

Inquiries with English groups suggest that there is a small but steady rise in the numbers of regular attenders at the cinema throughout adolescence and a drop in the small proportions of those who never attend. It seems that between 10 and 20 per cent. of adolescents attend regularly twice a week or more,[3]

---

[1] See Chapter VI.
[2] Marchant, *The Cinema in Education*, p. 47 (London, 1925).
[3] This figure is based on pre-war studies (1939). Recent data in the writer's possession suggest that the proportion of adolescents attending twice a week or more is considerably higher now (1947).

between 30 and 40 per cent. once a week, and the remainder once a month or sometimes. Barely 2 per cent. never go. Among boys, attendance seems to be slightly more frequent than among girls, and over twice as frequent among children of average and below average intelligence as among the more able grammar-school children[1]—though this may be because homework occupies much of the time of this latter group. There is evidence, too, which suggests that poorly adjusted children visit the films more frequently than normal, healthily developing boys and girls.[2]

Against the films many charges are brought—that they cause delinquency, have an over-stimulating effect upon the passions, or at least that they are bad for the eyes. It may be true that 'for the most part they give us not art but a show',[3] that the morality offered is crude, that the 'mass-produced film titillates what is bad and stupid in man: it ensures that dissatisfaction shall not burst into revolutionary action but shall fade away in dreams of a better world. It serves up in sugar coating what really needs combating.'[4] It is however doubtful whether the content of most films is on a lower level than that of women's magazine stories, of the Victorian or modern 'penny dreadful', the medieval ballad, or the ruck of popular drama of this or any preceding age. In the opinion of cautious investigators,[5] any connection between the cinema and delinquency among adolescents is very indirect. An excessive passion for the cinema (which may itself indicate maladjustment) may lead to thefts of money to pay for entrance; false values and stimulating scenes

[1] Jenkinson, op. cit., pp. 94–6, 237–8; Spencer, *School Children and the Cinema*, L.C.C., 1932.

[2] Hardy, 'The Out of School Activities of Well-Adjusted and Poorly-Adjusted Elementary School Pupils', *Journ. Ed. Psych.*, vol. xxvi, No. 6, 1935; Bannister and Ravden, 'The Environment and the Child', *B. Journ. P.*, vol. xxv, pt. 3, 1945; Carr-Saunders et al., loc. cit., p. 93.

[3] Morgan, op. cit., p. 85.

[4] Arnheim, *Film*, pp. 170–8 (London, 1933).

[5] Burt, *Young Delinquent*, pp. 143 ff.; Spencer, op. cit.; Ford, *Children in the Cinema*; E. Miller, article in *Sight and Sound*, No. 20, p. 132.

may precipitate a crisis in those who temperamentally or otherwise are already disposed to antisocial conduct. On the other hand, the realistic presentation of retribution overtaking a wrongdoer may, as one adolescent remarked, 'teach you that crime doesn't pay'.

This is not to say that the vivid realism of the cinema is entirely without effect. Other considerations suggest that the influence of films will be in proportion to the lack of experience of the viewer in the field with which they deal. To the adolescent boy or girl they are a source of fantasy material in the same way that novels and romances are. In their striking presentation of social techniques, of ways of behaving, of dress, hair style, and so on, they are a school in which the increasing self-consciousness of adolescents disposes them the more willingly to learn. The elaborate Payne Fund studies of the effect of the cinema provide ample evidence, from the accounts written by adolescents themselves, of their influence. For example, of 458 high-school girls, 62 per cent. acknowledge that films have given them ideas on how to dress, beautify themselves, or do their hair; and of the same group 33 per cent. admit that they tried to imitate the love technique of certain stars, sometimes with unfortunate results. Many, both children and adolescents, reported that their emotions had been aroused or stimulated by incidents seen on the screen, though the effect is usually short-lived. For example, 61 per cent. of the adolescents showed in their movie biographies, that a film had frightened or horrified them; 50 per cent. of girls and 26 per cent. of boys record that they have difficulty in controlling their crying in some films; and the investigators conclude that the emotions aroused by the portrayal of love and passion 'particularly when experienced by adolescents . . . are the most vivid form of emotional possession'. 'There is,' they write, 'ample indication that many high-school girls seek in such pictures a romantic love thrill, even though its setting be imaginative and vicarious. The repetition and accumulation of such experiences . . . seem quite important in stimulating, nurturing and organizing love impulses and amorous feelings.'[1]

Somewhat similar results were obtained by the writer from a group of 52 English boys and girls all between the ages of 14½ and 16. Though the vague phrase 'getting experience' occurred most frequently in answer to a question concerning the benefit derived from film-going, one girl wrote that the films 'teach you how to make love', another that she liked 'to watch their technique', and another 'they help one to learn the ways and means'. Apart from this, however, one must not neglect the motive of escape, of leaving behind for a space possibly drab or irksome home surroundings, of 'rest', 'change', 'something to do', and 'escape from boredom'; nor the mental attitude which underlies the remark, 'I prefer musical comedy because I like "happy ever after" endings and want to forget the troubles of the world for a while'. To some, however, musical films feed nascent, though ill formed and inarticulate, aesthetic interests. Such films, one girl writes, 'make one realize that there is beauty in the world', and another states that she goes 'for the joy of hearing some of the masterpieces from Handel or light opera parts'.

It may be said perhaps that the films appeal to much the same field of interests as does literature of all kinds and are as likely to be harmful or beneficial in their effects. Where the adolescent is equipped with developed critical attitudes, has a background of knowledge and experience, and is emotionally stable, cinema-going is unlikely to be excessive or harmful. It may in fact enlarge experience in a way which reading could never do. The danger lies in the fact that many films present to the inexperienced a set of values in which the stress is upon passive acceptance, upon crude sensationalism or upon ill-adaptive wish-

[1] Blumer, *Movies and Conduct*, pp. 31–33, p. 44; pp. 74 ff., pp. 98–9; p. 103; p. 107 (New York, 1933). See also the following: Blumer and Hausser, *Movies, Delinquency and Crime*; Dale, *The Content of Motion Pictures*.

fulfilment, and that, with the habit of reading literature of a good quality undeveloped, the screen may become the sole source of social, aesthetic, and emotional training. But for most even this danger can be over-estimated, Hard reality instils an awareness of the gulf between the silver screen and the drab street. The principal criticism which may be brought against the commercial cinema is, not that it corrupts, but that too many films miss the chance of elevating and refining public taste.

Aesthetic Impulses. In most researches into adolescence there are signs—especially towards the second half of the teens—of the development of aesthetic impulses. We have commented on this in connection with films. Table III shows that appreciable percentages, especially of girls, record increased interest in music, in making things, and in poetry, and a similar but more pronounced tendency is shown in the figures of Table IV, in which more than half of the student groups and rather more than a third (more men than women, interestingly enough) of the workers state that music, art, and poetry held increased interest for them in the teens.

The question of the psychological foundation of aesthetic emotions is a vexed one, bedevilled on the one hand by the highly subjective, metaphysical nature of much current aesthetic theory, and on the other by the difficulty which surrounds controlled experimentation. The evidence given by Margaret Phillips[1] suggests that experiences which would be recognized as aesthetic occur throughout life, correlated not so much with age as with the existence of surplus energy: as, however, the intelligence matures, it brings with it the ability to grasp more complex wholes. Adolescence, with its generally increased flow of emotional energy, and especially the latter half of the teens, is pre-eminently the time when emotion, intellect, and the desire to create unite with interests in nature, poetry, music,

[1] *The Education of the Emotions*, ch. vii (London, 1937).

visual art, drama, and so on to give an increased intensity to all sensuous experiences. Thus may grow either a genuine aesthetic sentiment: or, possibly because of inadequate teaching or of frustrations in other directions, a pseudo-aesthetic one, which finds in the jargon of this or that art the means of self-display, an emotional refuge, or an outlet for the fantasy life.

Experimental Learning. With most youths the motivation and expression of such interests are complex, compounded of many impulses, intellectual and emotional. With one, a dawning interest in nature may unite with a love of descriptive poetry and painting into a pantheism which finds food in the writings of the Lake poets and the English water-colourists. In another, scientific interests may provoke the avid reading of technical books, whilst an enthusiasm for jazz exists side by side with a craze for grand opera. Yet others, with a true aesthetic rapture or from a passion to win praise, may for a season engage in the practice of an art or craft. In another, reading, a passion for collecting, a roused curiosity and the desire to achieve technical perfection in drawing or photography, may unite in an amazing burst of productivity which leaves behind it a residual lifelong delight in visual expression.

Many of such activities are mere evanescent crazes, especially in the early teens when they provide an outlet for temporary conflicts. To the more stable adult, the boy or girl seems to be developing a butterfly mind which settles permanently nowhere; but rapid swings of interest, sharp enthusiasms, are a good rather than a bad sign. Too few interests may indicate an arrest of development, a poverty in the mental life or a self-absorption which prevents the outward flow of intellect and emotion to the environment. Changes in the field of interests must be regarded in the light of experimental learning, as the trying on of mental garments, until one or more are found to fit the growing mind; early specialization of interest is apt to be intense and narrow, too strait a jacket which cramps the spirit. The ideal would seem to be an ample range for experiment coupled with the discipline of some liberally conceived normative demands in the educational field, a training in carrying through some projects to the end, however bitter, along with the chance to follow a fleeting fancy in many fields. The sad thing is that for many adolescents the normative demands of school have ceased at fourteen, to be replaced by work which offers neither career nor vocation. The aroused interest in reading, in creative activity, in art, in nature, receiving neither stimulus from education, impetus from the environment, nor understanding from adults, spends itself on sentimentality and sensationalism, on newspaper verse, romances and thrillers from back-street shops, musical films of dubious aesthetic value, and crudities of taste in furniture, decorations, house-building and the like. It would be foolish to contend that the highest aesthetic and cultural development are open to the meanest intelligence; it is a counsel of despair and frustration to suggest that the stirrings of mentality in the teens cannot be moulded by education and opportunity to form the basis of a rich popular culture.

A Point of View. The interests and crazes of which we have been speaking in this and the preceding chapter are of critical importance to development. Not only may they indicate the future vocation of the adolescent or provide him with the relaxations of leisure in future years, but they give the material from which the youth will build a more or less conscious set of ideals, a moral and an ethical code. Very many think out no very comprehensive philosophy; they are content merely to accept the morality and principles of the group to which they belong, to conform to convention absorbed from the environment. The first brief weakly shoots of idealism meet perhaps with mockery or rebuff and a half-hearted cynicism is the result. A few never reach the mental level necessary to grasp the abstract concepts of right and wrong, of justice, truth, loyalty, honesty, and the like. In some rare spirits the struggle and the

9

mental torment begin early and continue long; reforming zeal, impulses of altruism, a desire for the abstract good of the human race, may blaze into a fierce dedication to a cause, a dedication which may be vexed with storms of doubt and feelings of utter unworthiness, or curiously alloyed with selfish ambition.

Religion. Not uncommonly this awakening to spiritual values takes the form of increased interest in religion; in some the typical phenomena of dramatic conversion may take place. Forty or fifty years ago this might have been considered the typical development, but in the last decades, religion as an interpretation of life has been accepted by a steadily decreasing proportion of people; nor has materialism or rationalism replaced it as a positive creed and our age may be described as one of unbelief rather than of disbelief.[1] This decay of religion inevitably has its effect upon the adolescent. The mechanistic materialism of science deprives the modern youth of a sense of personal importance in the scheme of things; but his ego is none the less rebellious against personal extinction. 'Modern man,' writes C. G. Jung,[2] 'Protestant or not, has lost the protection of the ecclesiastical walls carefully erected and reinforced since Roman days, and on account of that loss has approached the zone of world-destroying and world-creating fire.' It is perhaps to the existence of this void that we may attribute the readiness of youth to follow authoritarian political doctrines of the extreme left or extreme right. The only alternative seems to be the development of a personal religion, inside or outside the established creeds, an ethical code, and whatever explanation of life the individual can devise and accept emotionally. Such a spiritual evolution is likely to be more difficult than political or religious conversion; but its effects may well be more lasting, and at least equally valuable.

A reference to Table III will show that, even in the compara-

---

[1] Durant, *The Problem of Leisure,* p. 16 (London, 1938).
[2] *Psychology and Religion,* p. 59 (Yale Univ. Press, 1938).

tively early teens, over one-third of the group of normal adolescents record an intensification of their interest in religion, and
that 40 per cent. of boys and a quarter of the girls note a rising
interest in politics. In the more mature groups represented in
Table IV the proportions who claim to have had religious
experience are much higher except among the male workers, in
whom, possibly, though no evidence is provided, politics took
its place. It may be, as Hall[1] contends, that 'religion will always
hold as prominent a place in woman's life as politics does in
man's, and adolescence is still more its seed time with girls than
with boys'.

As in other things, religious or political conversion takes an
immense variety of forms. To a few, conversion comes as a
thunderclap, followed by an exaggerated introspection and
ritualism. 'I endured mental torture for a year due to introspection, making long lists of my sins and a conviction of my
worthlessness,' writes one girl. Others comment on a slow
growth or intensification of interest in the late teens. With
some, usually the more intellectual, religion or politics is merely
the form taken by vaguely formulated but sincere humanitarian
ideals; with others it is an intensely personal experience finding
expression in 'brooding, depression ... weeping, reading the
Holy Scriptures and self-inflicted tortures'.[2] In yet others the
approach may be primarily aesthetic, even in a sort mystical;
the music, ritual and solemnity of the church may arouse an
emotion never previously felt.

Whether conversion be sudden or slow, religious, ethical,
social-political or aesthetic, preceded or succeeded by a crisis
of doubt, self-distrust, or despair, whether it be superficial and
transitory or deep and lasting, will depend upon biological and
cultural factors, upon intelligence, emotionality, life experience,
and the formative influences operative at the time. It is however

[1] op. cit., p. 314.
[2] Hollingworth, *The Psychology of the Adolescent*, p. 188.

safe to say that few escape some quickening of the spiritual life.

In his study of religious conversion in the early years of this century, Starbuck[1] found that the great majority took place between the ages of twelve and twenty-five with peaks at twelve, sixteen, and nineteen. The average age for 'spontaneous awakening', 'a new life given to old beliefs, a new sense for God, a sudden delight in prayer', was about fourteen for girls and about two years later for boys. Slightly later but undoubtedly connected with this phenomenon is the opposing one of doubt. A research of Barnes[2] showed that for boys there is an early wave of doubt (probably stemming from the increased aggressiveness on which we commented in Chapter IV) culminating at fourteen or fifteen, followed by two or three years of comparative calm, and Starbuck's data, confirmed by Fritch and Hetzer's study of adolescent diaries,[3] demonstrate an even greater wave of doubt at or just before eighteen. For women the incidence of doubt, as that of conversion, is about two years earlier than for men.

The incidence and the intensity of adolescent conversion and religious fervour have been ascribed to the increasing power of the sex drive—as indeed has all religious emotion.[4] But, as Thouless[5] argues, it would be a mistake to attribute the awakening spiritual fervour of the adolescent solely to a sublimation of sexuality. Altruism and the change from the egocentricity of childhood, a desire to escape from the, at times overwhelming, aggressiveness of the early teens, 'the weight of too much liberty', the influence of persons in the environment, may all contribute. And, without the development of the intelligence at least to the point at which abstract concepts become possible and a train of reasoning can be followed to its conclusion, and

---

[1] *The Psychology of Religion*, p. 41.
[2] Cited by Pratt, *The Psychology of Religious Belief* (New York, 1908).
[3] Cited by Hollingworth, contrib. to *Handbook of Child Psychology*, p. 896.
[4] Freud, *The Future of an Illusion* (London, 1928).
[5] *Introduction to the Psychology of Religion*, pp. 131-4 (Cambridge, 1923).

without an intellectual sense of remoter ends, the problem of religion and of a personal philosophy will not arise.

An Interpretive Principle. This discussion of the intellectual developments of adolescence may perhaps be concluded by an attempt to formulate an interpretive principle. We have already seen that in the teens the intelligence reaches nearly to its maximum and at the same time special capacities and aptitudes declare themselves decisively. This puts at the disposal of the emotional life an intellectual instrument as good as it is likely to be. The development of aesthetic, altruistic, religious, or intellectual interests will be dependent upon the power of the intelligence and the constellation of special abilities; the strength with which they are felt, upon the level of general emotionality; and the form which they take, upon education, environment, and other social pressures. Many adolescents expect from religion, or philosophy, or political faith, a solution of their own personal conflicts; for them the moral and spiritual demands and the restrictions embodied in the church or in an authoritarian political creed represent the institutionalization of early parental authority, and form, as it were, a half-way stage in emancipation from the parents.[1] Others project their conflicts into the domains of philosophic discussion or find refuge in absorption in music, painting, poetry, the study of nature, or the pursuit of science. In some the aggressive tendencies are so powerful, and the emancipation from parental influences so difficult, that, for a time, there is a belligerent atheism, an energetic denial of values, which produces a painful but usually short-lived cynicism. A classic example of such development is that of Shelley, but his *Necessity of Atheism* could be paralleled in many a schoolboy essay. Such a phase, it seems, is commoner in boys than in girls.[2]

McDougall[3] has shown that on instinctive bases and as a

[1] Blos, *The Adolescent Personality*, pp. 296-7. Jones, 'The Psychology of Religion', *B. Journ. Med. P.*, vol. vi, pt. 4.
[2] Wheeler, op. cit., p. 73.
[3] McDougall, *Introduction to Social Psychology.*

result of incorporating influences from the environment, emotionally toned systems of ideas are built up throughout life. The maturation of intelligence in the teens means that, for the first time, many abstractions can be comprehended and incorporated—ideals of justice, truth, loyalty, unselfishness, morality, ethics—and the complex ideas which are essential to the developments of adequate sentiments for religion, art, politics, and so on come within the mental grasp. The relatively intense emotional activity of the period, the coincidence of puberty and the years which follow it, with important changes imminent or actual, in the individual's life, unite to sensitize the mind as never before to all kinds of environmental influences. The turning outwards of the mental life from the dependent egocentricity of childhood to the more maturely interdependent social orientation of the developed adult, gives a new direction to the old sentiments and forms the foundation for new. One may say that adolescence is pre-eminently the period in the life span when the whole character of the individual takes on a shape which may be later modified, but never radically changed. The formation of character depends upon the formation of sentiments; strength of character is built upon their integration into a hierarchy under the dominance of an adequate master sentiment of the self. In these malleable years the boy and girl have to find their level in relation to others, and have somehow to reconcile conflicting aspects of their nature into a harmonious union.

Freud has pointed to the effects both on action and on thinking of emotional dispositions which, because of their incompatibility with the ideals of the conscious life, have become repressed, thrust down into the unconscious mind, and inaccessible to introspection. Some desires must be repressed; but by adequate training and guidance, by offering opportunities for the redirection of the instinctive forces which prompt them, they need not breed pestilence in the unconscious. If urgent, unsatisfied needs remain in the youth, or conflicts are left unresolved, energy is absorbed which might be applied to the business of living. Where this is extreme, we get the exhaustion states of so-called neurasthenia; but, even in a mild form, frustration and conflict thwart the growth of character, warping the sentiments and perhaps preventing the growth of the most worth-while.

The aim of education—and in this home, school, and society each has a part to play—must be to provide, through books, music, and art, through vital experience and the example of fine personalities, and through the satisfaction of fundamental needs, the materials and the necessary conditions for the growth of the most comprehensive sentiments of which the growing boy or girl is capable. No society can afford to be indifferent to the fact that any group or organization which makes the youth feel himself necessary to others is in a peculiarly strong position to influence his growth and through the sentiment it inspires permanently to shape his outlook on life. The cultural unity of the primitive tribe allowed the one initiation and indoctrination of the pubic ceremonial. Certainly until the middle nineteenth century—even for many to-day—institutionalized religion offered a framework within which to formulate a more or less personal philosophy. Scientific materialism, the shock of two major wars in a generation, and the chaos of values, virtues, and morals which we see about us now, make the quest for a satisfying point of view free of doubts exceedingly difficult. Literature, radio, personal precept and example, the cinema, the churches, offer discordant values. Education should not impose a code, however well chosen, but offer techniques and guiding principles and provide a breathing-space for experiment. Thus each boy and girl according to his or her needs and abilities, may select the materials from which to build a satisfying and personal interpretation of life, moral, ethical, or religious.

CHAPTER VI

LEARNING TO LIVE

I. HAS POPULAR EDUCATION FAILED?

Illiteracy. More than fifty years of free, universal, and compulsory education, although it has achieved much, has not succeeded in making us an educated and cultured nation. On the basis of studies carried out before the recent war, Burt[1] estimated that at the age of sixteen 1 per cent. of all boys and girls are illiterate—that is, unable to make any use whatever of reading and writing; and that a further 10 per cent. are semi-literate—that is, unable to write an intelligible letter or to read more than the headlines of the simpler newspapers. Between the ages of sixteen and twenty-five, the proportions increase to between 1½ and 2 per cent. illiterate and 15 to 20 per cent. semi-literate. The upheaval of the recent war is not likely to have lessened these numbers. In 1943 the present writer[2] tested a representative group of 135 boys and girls, all of whom had left elementary schools within the previous year or two and all of whom were normal or dull-normal in intelligence. They were, in fact, representative of about two-thirds of our population. Of this group half were educationally backward all round. In the fundamental processes of arithmetic, they were retarded on the average one educational year in addition, two in subtraction, and more than three in multiplication and division. From a simple piece of concrete description, more than half the group

---

[1] 'The Education of Illiterate Adults', *B. Journ. Ed. P.*, vol. xv, pt. 1, 1945.

[2] 'The Decay of Educational Attainments among Adolescents', *B. Journ. Ed. P.*, vol. xiv, pt. 1, 1944.

were unable to gather five out of fifteen salient facts. Words like 'gutted' and 'consumption', phrases such as 'starting off on the wrong foot', and the least trace of irony, however obvious, were beyond the comprehension and outside the experience of any but the brightest.

Educational Interests. Inevitably such a poor grasp of the essentials of education will hinder developments in other fields. Table V shows the results of an inquiry[1] with a very similar group of 45 boys and 90 girls, all of them aged between fourteen and sixteen and all products of elementary schools. Each was asked to indicate his or her attitude to a number of 'subjects' such as might be included in the curriculum of a Day Continuation School or Youth College. Within this somewhat limited field of topics, there is little unanimity of interests. There is no subject liked 'very much' or 'quite well' by two-thirds of the boys, and only four (cookery, dancing, music, and typing) by two-thirds of the girls; and there is little or no overlap between the sexes. The figures in the fourth column which show the proportions of the group who dislike the twenty-eight activities offered are a shrewd index of the failure of education to make an appeal to such youth.

The table brings out strikingly the practical and non-verbal nature of the preferences of both girls and boys of this particular intellectual and educational background. In the boys' list there is no subject into which verbal mastery enters to any great extent, though the characteristic sex preferences for number and mechanical things are much in evidence. In the girls' list, though in view of the known verbal superiority of girls one might have expected differently, there is a similar predominance of practical, non-verbal, activities. The only subjects which could be said to have a marked verbal bias are two of a vocational nature—

[1] Wall, 'The Educational Interests of a Group of Young Industrial Workers', *B. Journ. Ed. P.*, vol. xv, pt. 3, 1935. The author wishes to acknowledge the permission given by the editor of the above journal to quote extensively from the article in what follows.

TABLE V

Distribution of Educational Preferences in a Group of 135 Adolescent Industrial Workers

	Liked very much per cent.		Liked quite well per cent.		Would join in per cent.		Disliked per cent.	
	Boys	Girls	Boys	Girls	Boys	Girls	Boys	Girls
1 Cookery	0	53	0	24	0	12	100	10
2 Needlework and Dressmaking	0	34	0	29	0	16	100	21
3 Embroidery	0	19	0	29	0	26	100	26
4 Art (that is design, painting, painting china, modelling, etc.)	0	11	15	14	11	21	73	53
5 Dancing—of all kinds	20	71	2	19	4	3	73	7
6 Keep-fit—rhythmic exercises and games	20	30	29	19	4	16	47	36
7 Dramatics (reading and acting plays, making costumes, props, etc.)	0	11	0	13	7	32	93	43
8 Making and Working a Puppet Theatre	0	2	2	4	11	20	87	73
9 Producing a Newspaper or Magazine	2	0	7	10	7	17	84	73
10 Home Craft and Household Science (electrical gadgets, gas and other fuels, laundry work, etc.)	4	1	7	10	16	20	73	69
11 Discussion Circle on any topic of interest (e.g. films, wireless, etc.)	7	1	11	8	20	22	62	69

#		4	38	7	29	13	18	76	16[1]
12	Music—from swing to classics	4	2	7	7	9	14	78	77
13	Learning about living creatures, especially ourselves	7	44	2	21	4	9	91	26
14	Shorthand	2	54	4	14	4	9	89	22
15	Typing	2	22	0	30	4	23	93	24
16	First-aid, Home Nursing, etc.	2	14	0	8	9	26	91	52
17	Hygiene	0							
18	Handicrafts of various kinds, (woodwork, metal work, rug-making, leather-work, and so on)	44	11	18	24	9	17	29	48
19	Workshop Drawing	22	0	24	0	22	8	31	92
20	The use of Workshop Tools	27	1	36	0	18	6	20	93
21	Studying various mechanisms (petrol, steam, oil, etc.)	47	1	11	0	16	6	27	93
22	Reading and Discussing *any* books brought by members	7	1	4	10	7	27	82	62
23	Workshop Calculations	33	0	24	0	20	6	22	94
24	Arithmetic	24	2	27	9	18	21	31	68
25	Letter Writing	0	9	11	22	16	19	73	50
26	Elocution	4	17	7	17	13	18	76	49
27	Study of Local Conditions (industry, housing, government, etc.)	4	2	9	0	13	18	73	80
28	Modern History	2	2	20	7	9	11	69	80

typing and shorthand—in which manual and perceptual skills are paramount, and dramatics, which relies for its appeal, not perhaps primarily upon its verbal element, but upon impulses of display and identification with adult characters.

If those subjects which are disliked by 50 per cent. or more of each group are examined, two other tendencies are discernable. There seems to be a disinclination to take up those activities which are unfamiliar to the average elementary-school child (for example, Nos. 8, 9, and 11). In part at least, this confirms the observation of Wray and Fergusson,[1] who comment upon the aversion shown by the average adolescent worker to live thinking. In part, it may be a fear of the new and of failing in the attempt, for, if any characteristic is outstanding in the make-up of such children as these, it is their poor educational morale. The second tendency is a distaste for those subjects in the elementary-school curriculum in which they have had little demonstrable success (for example Nos. 4, 13, 25, and 27). The entire absence from the boys' list and the scanty representation in the girls' of any subject of aesthetic appeal is striking, and there is in neither any indication that social or political awareness has been roused at school.

These facts are a severe indictment of education as it has been conceived so far—at least in our elementary schools. On the basis of the figures given at the beginning of this chapter it seems that there cannot be less than 2¼ million illiterate and semi-literate adults in our population at present.[2] That there are more is probable since, among weak readers who are not technically semi-literate, there may be a gap of as much as two or more educational years between their ability to translate printed symbols into spoken words and their power to understand what they laboriously construe.[3]

---

[1] *A Day Continuation School at Work*, p. 15 (Longmans, 1920).
[2] Burt, loc. cit.
[3] Wall, 'Reading Backwardness among Army Men', pts. 1 and 2.

Two Races of Men. More serious even than this, socially and politically, are the signs that in our society two races of men are growing up—a dwindling few to whom words, spoken or written, are the instruments of thought, and who hold discourse still to be 'man's noblest attribute'; and an increasing many who can be appealed to only through the eye. The immense popularity of magazines with the maximum of pictures and the minimum of letterpress, the circulation of 'newspapers' which consist of photographs and comic strips with a modicum of potted comment, and the figure of 18½ million attendances weekly at the cinema are evidence that

> . . . prose and verse, sunk into disrepute
> Must lacquey a dumb art that best can suit
> The taste of this once intellectual land.

Nor can it be said that among a large proportion of those educated in our secondary grammar schools is the spirit of informed curiosity alive. How many of these will admit quite frankly that they 'had enough of that at school' when the higher pleasures of the mind come under discussion?

Causes. Backwardness in the tool subjects of education has been the subject of considerable investigation in recent years. Children whose intelligence quotient is below 85, more or less inevitably, have a lower standard of achievement than the average, though with adequate teaching methods suited to their more limited ability, all but the dullest can achieve a useable standard of literacy. Defective powers of visual or auditory analysis, specific defects in imagery—for example, the boy who cannot visualize words or who cannot 'hear' sounds in his mind—and weakness in short- or long-term recall, can, if undetected and not met by special remedial training, hamper or prevent the acquisition of the 'three R's'. So too, defective vision, hearing, or speech, weakness in neuromuscular control, poor physical tone, irregular attendance at school, in fact any hindrance or handicap, especially in the critical early years, may operate singly or in combination as a contributory or more rarely as a primary cause.[1]

Emotional Difficulties. We have already discussed the close connection between emotional difficulties and educational failure; and there seems to be no reason to doubt that temperamental defects are in some cases the cause of backwardness and distaste for school. In others, a failure in the early stages of learning to read may give rise to a persistent emotional disturbance, the results of which react upon school progress in a cumulative way, and carry over into adult life not merely as poor educational morale but as a gesture of despair and self-distrust which eventually develops into neurosis. The present writer found[2] that of a group of one hundred illiterate and semi-literate adults, nearly two-thirds were suffering from disturbances in their emotional life which would be called neurotic. Whether because of this or because of the mere rusting of basic skills, the backward school child tends to become the more backward adolescent and the still more backward adult; as time wears on the gap between potentiality, as represented by intelligence, and educational achievement increases, especially in those whose abilities are lowest.

Dislike for School. These are the most serious cases, most of whom, even when their special handicaps are met by specially devised methods, will not achieve more than a limited mastery of verbal and arithmetic tools. But for many children whose attainment reaches a satisfactory level without special assistance, it seems that school holds no compelling attraction in the teens. Questioning elementary-school leavers in East London, King[3] found that nearly three-quarters of them had no further use for school at all. Only half of a group of 323 men all educationally normal questioned by the present writer stated that they looked

[1] Burt, *The Backward Child*; Schonell, *Backwardness in the Basic Subjects* (London, 1942).
[2] loc. cit., p. 124.
[3] *The Employment and Welfare of Juveniles* (London, 1926).

back on school with any pleasure; 17 per cent. had actively disliked it, and another third had been indifferent.[1]

Some of this distaste is due to the prolongation of childhood status, appropriate perhaps in earlier years, into the teens; some of it to a lack of reality and satisfaction in the curriculum; much of it to the mistake of presenting material prematurely to the boy or girl. This last, though a grievous mistake, has been excusable when the school life ended at fourteen; but Shakespeare or Shelley thrust in now-or-never mood down unwilling throats teaches nothing but disgust, bewilderment, and failure. The crises in the instinctive life of the early teens also, for which few of our schools have made allowances, and the complete failure of most of our curricula to provide emotional education, must bear no small part of the blame.

The Community. We cannot however lay the responsibility entirely upon the schools. Undoubtedly very many of them have been isolated from the life of the community, playing little part in it, and with their eyes fixed rather upon the past than upon the present or the future. But there is much justice in the criticism that 'the community which they enter is often unworthy of the young people who may come from a soundly run school with high aims and a reasonably satisfactory attitude towards work, and find themselves in adult groups where the main aim among the unambitious is to get out of as much work as possible and among the more ambitious 'to get on in the world', the criterion of success being the amount of earnings'. These are but aspects of a self-perpetuating vicious circle. School and community interact. If the school can offer no sincere conception of the good life which should be led, it is unlikely to arise spontaneously in the majority when school is left behind. On the other hand, it is difficult for the schools to offer a coherent set of values set over against a world in chaos.[2]

[1] Unpublished material.
[2] *Memorandum for the Central Advisory Council for Education* (England), prepared by the A.T.C.D.E. *Bulletin of Education*, July 1946.

II. EDUCATION FOR THE ADOLESCENT
AND THE 1944 ACT

The Effects of the War. Society has been slow to recognize the folly of ceasing educational provision in the early formative years of adolescence. The first few years of the recent war, however, with their heightened tension, disruption of home life, and high wages for juveniles in industry, threw a sharper light upon the problems presented by boys and girls in their teens, and the public conscience awoke to the fact that a generation might be cast away before our eyes. The war however merely intensified symptoms which were obvious to the discerning in between the wars, speeding up a disruptive process which, if allowed to continue, must inevitably mean that at least half our community will arrive at the age of suffrage insufficiently literate to grasp even the simpler issues involved.

The Youth Movement. One result of the stirring of a social conscience has been a great expansion in the organizations which provide leisure occupations for adolescents and the change of emphasis from merely preventive to constructive activities. It is estimated that in 1939 in Nottinghamshire,[1] less than 15 per cent. of boys and girls between the ages of fourteen and eighteen were members of youth organizations. By 1942 these figures had risen to 46 per cent. of boys and 17 per cent. of girls; and in 1944 the proportions had reached 52 per cent. of boys and 46 per cent. of girls. Much of this increase, doubtless, is due to enrolment in pre-service units of one kind or another and the compelling motive which this represents has largely passed with the return of peace. We may expect that, even with the most favourable conditions, the membership of all kinds of voluntary youth organizations will not exceed 60 per cent. of the 14–18 age group and will probably be less.[2]

[1] Barnes, *Youth Service in an English County,* King George's Jubilee Trust, 1945
[2] This agrees with Kitchen's estimate of the proportions of adolescents who would voluntarily join in spare-time educational activities; see *From Learning to Earning,* p. 42.

The value of a good club to the development of boys or girls cannot be overestimated. It gives the opportunity for largely unsupervised activities, and should throw the onus of organization, government, and responsibility on to the adolescent. It offers the chance for informal education, providing a wider background than the home can give, and a less formal one than most schools. With all these and other advantages, the club can yet be only an auxiliary in the education of the growing youth. It is neither just nor practical to expect the efforts of club leaders and young people themselves to provide in meagre leisure time all the training that so critical a period of development demands.

School leaving. Prior to 1939, three-quarters of our boys and girls left full-time education at the age of fourteen to enter shops, offices, and factories in the dawning years of adolescence. Of the remainder, about half—and those the best favoured by nature or circumstances—continued in some kind of full-time educational provision at least until mid-adolescence at the age of sixteen; and the rest pursued part-time study either on one day a week or in the evenings after a day's work. The Fisher Act, passed at the end of World War I, was an attempt to remedy some of these inequalities and injustices by, among other things, the establishment of universal part-time education for several years after the end of the full-time school life. Rugby alone has retained compulsory part-time day continuation education, and some enlightened firms have set up schools of a similar nature for their young employees; but public opinion generally was insufficiently enlightened to prevent the Fisher Act from passing into abeyance in the interests of short-sighted economy.

The Education Act, 1944. The 1944 Education Act is a bold step forward. Under its provisions, education is to be organized in three consecutive stages: (*a*) the period before the beginning of compulsory school life, for which there is to be a greater provision of nursery schools and classes, with an emphasis on health and social training; (*b*) the period of childhood, for which the common Junior or Primary school is to cater up to the dawn of puberty; and (*c*) the period of Secondary Education, extending full-time to fifteen (and later to sixteen), and followed by at least part-time education to the age of eighteen. There are a great many other provisions in the Act, which has been described as 'the greatest and grandest educational advance this country has ever made'.[1] From our present point of view, the most important thing is that, for the first time in our history, the period of adolescence is recognized for *all* children, and not only for the favoured minority, as primarily of educational significance. By the abolition of fees for secondary education, by a greater provision of maintenance grants, and by an extension of the school meals and medical services, much has been done to ensure that it is so and that all children in truth have that equality of educational opportunity which we have never had in the past.

Variety of Provision. A natural corollary of the extension of secondary education to all adolescents is a variety of provision to meet the needs of differing types of child, and the obligation laid on parents and public authorities to see that each boy and girl receives the kind of education for which he or she is best fitted. On the precise kinds of curriculum and school which are to be set up, the Act is, rightly, vague. Much experiment and clear thinking will be required in the next decade, before we can be finally committed to anything but a very flexible scheme. Most education authorities are, however, following the general lines suggested in the Norwood Report on the *Curriculum and Examinations in Secondary Schools*,[2] which in itself embodies suggestions made in the earlier Hadow and Spens Reports on

---

[1] H. C. Dent, *A Landmark in English Education*, p. 7 (London, 1943).
[2] H.M.S.O., 1943. See also *The Education of the Adolescent* [Hadow Report]. (H.M.S.O., 1921). *Secondary Education: Grammar Schools and Technical High Schools* [Spens Report] (H.M.S.O., 1936).

education for the adolescent.[1] The Norwood Report proposes three principal types of secondary provision—Grammar, Technical, and Modern. Of these, the first is intended for 'the pupil who is interested in learning for its own sake, who can grasp an argument or follow a piece of connected reasoning'. The second—Secondary Technical education—is to cater for those 'whose interests and abilities lie markedly in the field of applied Science or applied Art'. The third—that to be provided in Secondary Modern Schools or courses—is to be suitable for the pupil 'who deals more easily with concrete things than with ideas'.

The neatness of this categorization appeals more to the administrator than to the psychologist who recognizes the difficulty of selecting children on the basis of special aptitudes at the early age of eleven or twelve. Further, in spite of what the Norwood Report says explicitly to the contrary, these divisions correspond much more to what we know of levels of general intelligence than to any distinction of psychological types.[2] Provided however that the administrative framework is not, in practice, rigidly based upon such arbitrary classifications of pubescent and pubertal children, and provided that there is ample opportunity for children to transfer from one kind of educational provision to another without disadvantage, the scheme proposed may work satisfactorily.

The Multilateral School. In practice, the best solution seems to be the establishment of the Multilateral School which shall cater for a cross-section of adolescents of all levels of ability and aptitude. Such a school can provide a common curriculum, treated at different levels of difficulty, during the first year or two of adolescence, followed later by a number of increasingly diverging special courses. This is the solution proposed by the

[1] Though it ignores much of the evidence, especially of psychologically trained witnesses, on which the earlier reports were based.
[2] Burt, 'The Education of the Adolescent: The Psychological Implications of the Norwood Report', *B. Journ. Ed. P.*, vol. xiii, pt. 3, 1943.

L.C.C.: and that it is practicable where numbers are large enough and buildings available is shown by the success of the well-known Kirkcaldy High School.[1] The method has many advantages. It ensures that 'parity of esteem' for the differing types of provision which is rightly considered of great importance. It enables specialization to be delayed until aptitudes and vocational aims are readily detectable; and it allows of transfer from one kind of course to another with the minimum of disturbance. It has too the great advantage that children of differing interests and abilities are educated together, to the advantage of all.

Certain arguments have been urged against the Multilateral School. The most serious is, that to cater efficiently for the wide range of individual variation, the school must accommodate upwards of 900 pupils—some say 1,200 or more. These numbers are too large to allow an intimate and personal atmosphere without special measures being taken. In areas of scattered population, moreover, it may well be impossible to obtain large enough concentrations of children for a multilateral school without many of them having either to live on the premises or travel for long distances. The Act encourages experiment of all kinds to meet local conditions, and various modifications of the multilateral idea—combinations of grammar and modern secondary courses, of technical and grammar courses, for example—have been proposed and will be tried out in the next few years.

County Colleges. An equally important section of the Act is that referring to part-time education after the ending of compulsory full-time schooling at the age of fifteen (later sixteen). The years from then until the age of eighteen, which, as we have seen, are of crucial importance in mental development, will be regarded for most as a period of adjustment to the working life, a tapering off of compulsory education. All

[1] Earle, *Reconstruction in the Secondary School* (London, 1944).

adolescents, not otherwise catered for, will be required to spend in educational activities at least one day of each week for forty-four weeks of the year (or two continuous periods of a month or one continuous period of two months). To meet the needs of such adolescents, County Colleges are to be set up within three years of the date of the raising of the school-leaving age (i.e. in 1950) with the declared objects of providing, as the Act itself says, such 'physical, practical, and vocational training as will enable them to develop their various aptitudes and capacities and will prepare them for the responsibilities of citizenship'.[1]

We now have the administrative framework—with a few shortcomings here and there—for a truly democratic and child-centred system of education. In the past too many children have been educational misfits, either because a high economic valuation was set upon one type of secondary education, or because the child was looked on as a lump of raw material which could be moulded to any shape if only the pressure were hard and continuous enough. Apart from the inefficiency and unhappiness revealed by the figures cited at the beginning of the chapter, it has been calculated that not less than 40 per cent. of our most able children have in the past failed to receive the education for which they were best fitted.[2] Now, there is no legal impediment to prevent any child being educated truly for life. Success will depend upon teachers, administrators, parents, and public opinion. It will depend upon a clear realization by them of the goals of individual development, on a sure knowledge of the laws governing growth in all its aspects, and on an intelligent awareness that the kind of education which we give our children and adolescents will shape the whole future social and spiritual structure of our society.

Educational Needs of a Democracy. We have insufficient

[1] *Youth's Opportunity*, Min. of Ed. Pamphlet No. 3 (H.M.S.O., 1945).
[2] Burt, 'Ability and Income', *B. Journ. Ed. P.*, vol. xiii, pt. 2, 1943.

space here to discuss in detail all the kinds of provision which will be necessary. We can however now attempt a synthesis between what is known of adolescent developments and adolescent needs on the one hand, and on the other the demands of society. Fortunately there are many answers to the question, 'What is the best education for the adolescent?' and it is from them that will spring the rich diversity of personalities which is the strength of a free and evolving community. We may, however, be agreed on certain desirables in society itself, a clear definition of which will give clarity to our educational aims. The democratic way of life implies the complete legal and political equality of all men and women: it implies too the right to develop all one's powers and aptitudes within the social framework and encourages independence of development, freedom of thought, personal—rather than collective or central —responsibility, and the inviolability of the personal conscience. Of necessity, it involves the clash of views on all important issues, a recognition of the binding nature of majority decisions and yet the protection of minority rights. It involves revolution by persuasion, and tolerance preserved in the teeth of passion. This demands of the citizen a vigilant and critical mind, some sense of social purpose, and a responsiveness to issues other than purely personal ones. A full realization of the ideals of democracy is impossible, too, without a cultural unity in the nation which cannot come to pass if there are social distinctions in education; if rich and poor, able and less able, spend their educational life in watertight compartments with different ethics and objectives.

These requirements imply that in each, the power of critical thinking should be developed to the full capacity allowed by native endowment and, as a necessary instrument, the power of communication in words. Such a training will be useless unless it includes the ability to discern the ways in which emotion may interfere with reason, a knowledge of the limitations of one's own powers of analysis, and of the point at which judgement should be suspended. Suggestibility and contra-suggestibility—the readiness to believe everything one is told or the unwillingness to believe anything—must be dissipated by an adequate body of knowledge and by practice in finding information from unbiased and objective sources. Hence education must develop curiosity in all directions rather than sate or destroy it in some or all, and it must concentrate upon educating a personality rather than a mind or body, on ethical and emotional development as well as on the acquisition of skills.

Adolescent Learning. The child is often prepared to accept the need for learning simply on the prestige of the teacher. The adolescent questions the utility of studies. He desires to know whither they tend and of what use they are likely to be. If the teacher knows not the answer or does not live it in his own life, a natural result is loss of interest. The content of the education offered to youth must be demonstrably connected with the world as it is; the school must in truth be a school for life. Otherwise we get the sorry spectacle of the boy or girl forced to stew at this or that because of an alleged cultural or disciplinary value and gaining in the process nothing but a stultified curiosity and a mass of inert ideas. We must for ever cast out the idea, implicit in so many of our curricula, that 'knowledge by *suffering* entereth'. Adolescent education must be founded on the adult motives for learning—interest, reality, and clearly presented and worth-while goals.

Education must, too, be a whole process, not a matter of imparting information for so many hours a day, attending societies in fag-ends of leisure time and leaving all the rest to chance and the influence of the home. School, home, and community must somehow be brought into a clear and unequivocal integration. This can be done by a change of attitude on the part of some teachers and some parents, who should come together, not merely on a social basis, but for the more serious purposes of community life. It can be done too by a deliberate orientation of the school to the facilities and needs of the neighbourhood. Only in this way can the growing child be offered a coherent set of values, a sincere conviction that the good life can be led. We must not accept the position that, by paying teachers to instruct our children, we have abrogated either our right to influence education or our duty to integrate its products with the adult life that flows round the schools.

The Syllabus. Such ideas imply that the syllabus must be directed forward and outward. To use the modern phrase, it must provide a series of 'fields of activity' progressively co-ordinated with a clear aim in view—that of allowing each growing mind to frame for itself answers to the questions which beset it. It must develop techniques of analysis and synthesis, modes of behaviour ranging from personal good manners to that consideration for others which bids us clarify our own thinking before it finds expression in words. Facts can always be found if we know where to look for them; the ability to handle and manipulate them is something to be laboriously trained. It is on the distillation of wisdom, and not alone on the gathering of scattered petals of learning that right living depends.[1]

English. The pitiful inarticulateness of so many adults who, to express their deepest emotions must mouth the words of a popular song or who are mesmerized by publicists' slogans, suggests that the core of education should be the mother tongue. Clarity and precision of speech and writing, the use of English as an instrument of thought, comprehension of the printed word as a means of obtaining information, should all be made focal points of teaching in the early teens.

This does not mean the continual working of arid examples in correct speech or dull comprehension exercises. The teacher should seize upon the experience provided by the cinema, the

[1] In what follows the writer is indebted to the *Interim Report of the Council for Curriculum Reform* (London, 1945) and *General Education in a Free Society*, Report by Harvard Committee (Cambridge, Mass., 1946).

desire to make things, the rising interest in nature, in collecting, and so on, and show how these may be forwarded by a command of English. The working instructions for making a model aeroplane, a cookery recipe, a dress pattern, provide real occasions for exercising comprehension. So too a systematized collection of postage stamps, fossils, wild flowers, birds' eggs, photographs, or anything else can readily lead to some instruction in the use of the library and of works of reference. Debates and discussions on real topics of lively importance to the pupils themselves ('the advantages or otherwise of good manners'— 'should boys and girls be allowed to stay out late?'—'a vote for sixteen-year-olds?') are training in oral expression, lead to a definition of ideas, and may, suitably guided, awaken a conscious desire for that precision in thinking which leaves no loophole for an opponent.

Literature. English too may be the vehicle for emotional education. Novels, biographies, poetry, all portray life, in which the adolescent is supremely interested. Everything here depends upon the books which are placed before the youth. No book should be included simply because it has been acclaimed a masterpiece, but primarily because it deals faithfully with personal, emotional, or intellectual issues on the level of development of the boy or girl who is to read it and because of the satisfaction it offers to the developing instinctive and fantasy life. This does not prevent the teacher from using inspirational methods, from communicating his own enthusiasms, provided he does not insist upon all his recommendations being immediately followed. On one occasion, in an access of enthusiasm, the writer recommended a class of fourteen-year-olds to read the *Religio Medici*! The suggestion passed unfollowed at the time. Years later he heard from one of the pupils in that class that he had just got round to Sir Thomas Browne and was, at the age of twenty-five, about to follow the suggestion made eleven years earlier.

Modern literature is more likely to appeal, especially in the early teens, than that in which the customs, fashions, conventions, and language of the past add to the difficulties of interpretation. Best of all are those few great and simple masterpieces which appeal to different emotions and interests at different ages and can thus be used as a bridgehead from which other literary adventures can begin. Poems such as *The Ancient Mariner* or *Flannan Isle*, books like *Little Women*, *Treasure Island*, or *Jim Davis*, are an admirable nucleus. Nor should the magazines, the bloods and comics beloved of boys and girls, be spoken of in shocked disgust. It is doubtful whether they are more crude than the ballads which are now considered meet food for the young; and they can be used with caution as stepping-stones to more complex and subtle literary expressions. Drama, particularly plays like *Junior Miss*, *Dear Octopus*, *Pygmalion*, and the plays which boys and girls adapt themselves from novels and short stories, may serve many purposes in mental development. It can be used to socialize the love of self-display, to provide means and models of behaviour, and to act as an emotional catharsis for personal conflicts and preoccupations.

The English Subjects. According to the needs, background, and attainments of the group, the scope of English teaching may and should be extended over what one might call the English subjects with an increasing emphasis on content, on information and its systematization into a coherent and useful body of knowledge. History and geography in their human and social aspects, in their bearing upon life and thought, upon politics and foreign affairs, may be thus approached. The question of what should be included must be answered according to the criterion of relevance to the lives, present and future, of the pupils. Hence a study of the history, geology, topography, industry, social and administrative framework of the district in which the school is situated is likely to mean more and to teach more to the adolescent than is a bare list of the products of Indo-China or the political history of medieval Europe.

Science. Many inquiries have shown the interest of boys and girls in scientific and particularly in biological facts. Life in the modern world demands from every man and woman a degree of technical knowledge unknown before the industrial revolution. There are signs—the popularity of palmists and astrologers and the sales of lucky charms for example—that superstition is on the increase. The basic syllabus therefore must find a place for a grounding in those aspects of physics, mechanics, and biology which have a direct human and contemporary bearing. It is worth remembering that objective scientific facts, things in themselves unemotional, and the neat conclusive logicality of the demonstration of a natural or mathematical law, are for many a present refuge when the emotional life reaches a disturbing intensity. Such a study of science should aim to answer the philosophic questions which arise in the teens, to provide the knowledge necessary to understand implements of daily use, to fortify against superstition, and to give a basis upon which the technological advances of our civilization can be comprehended.

Creative Work. The treatment of the emotionally disturbed in recent years has drawn attention to the therapeutic value of handicrafts as a means of relieving tension. In itself this would be a sufficient justification for their inclusion in the syllabus. The additional satisfaction of making something, of conclusively demonstrating to oneself (and others) one's own competence, is also not to be despised. The attempt to create, which should be integral to the teaching of all subjects whether manual or verbal, lays the basis on which aesthetic appreciation may be built later. A word of caution is however necessary. We must remember that the finer muscular co-ordinations are often disturbed in the early stages of puberty and that on this account, too high a standard of execution in embroidery, drawing, and so on cannot be expected. Coupled with the increasing self-consciousness and self-criticism of the period this not infrequently leads the boy or girl to turn away from the more subtle and delicate techniques to the broader constructive work involved in such activities as carpentry, rug-making, weaving, and leather work. Such occupations should not be provided as a despised alternative or 'soft options' for those who cannot make adequate progress in more intellectual studies. They should be an essential and considerable part of the curriculum for all adolescents. The words

>I too will something make
>And joy in the making

can become for all a living reality, which should last the rest of their lives.

Physical Education. The tables of Chapter V drew attention to the interest of large numbers, of both sexes and of all degrees of mental capacity, in strenuous physical activity. On this may be founded the physical education of the adolescent. Organized group games—played not by the expert few only—and systematic exercises designed to meet anomalies of development and to ensure harmony of muscular control are of importance. Equally essential, though at present often overlooked, are the more social aspects of physical development—dancing for example, and the art of graceful movement. And the whole should be rounded off with a knowledge of dietetics, of the rules of physical health and of hygiene. Making the most of the physical self must be recognized as being as legitimate an object as making the best use of the mind: physical harmony is one of the bases of emotional concord.

Aesthetic Education. The second phase of adolescence, when the tumult in the instinctive life has calmed down somewhat, and when the pressing need for new avenues of expression has passed, when the adolescent is more sure of himself and less absorbed in the acquisition of modes of behaviour, is the period for laying the foundations of a wider cultural and aesthetic education on which the adult can build. Music, poetry, painting, architecture, not to be neglected in the earlier stages, are unlikely to have had any purely aesthetic appeal. At sixteen or seventeen they may be discovered by the youth with all the dazzling suddenness of conversion.[1] When the emotional life is thoroughly ripe for them they can come to exercise a dominating influence and place in the curriculum. If they have been prematurely pressed upon the attention of boys and girls with a categorical 'I think these are good for you and you must learn them', they will be passed by on the other side when school is left behind—as indeed is the case with melancholy frequency among people to-day.

Increasing Specialization. The basic core of studies outlined above is infinitely adaptable to the needs of the individual child. Much can and should be added to meet vocational and intellectual aims. Quite early in the teens the child of high ability will be ready for systematized bodies of knowledge delighted in for their own sake, and, for such, the more or less compartmented syllabus of the academic grammar school is not unsuitable. Even here, however, there is room for a reconstruction and reorientation of the syllabus, an expansion of the time devoted to some subjects and a drastic reduction in the hours spent on others, especially as special abilities and constellations of aptitudes begin to declare themselves. The boy or girl who, in the mid-teens, displays special mechanical, scientific, or technical ability and begins to form a vocational ambition which renders a special kind of education appropriate, should be allowed to add more specific studies to the programme. To others, the humanities will make a special appeal. For others, and those the majority, training of a general kind but with real relationship to the field of employment open to them, is a suitable addition—office routine, filing, shorthand, typewriting,

[1] Margaret Phillips, *The Education of the Emotions*, ch. viii and ix.

book-keeping, the compilation of simple statistics, the economics of industry and retail trade, the history of the Trade Union movement, the broad outlines of industrial and social legislation.

Religion. A word must be said about the place of religion in the education of the adolescent. It is a subject on which unbiased thinking free of dogmatic assertions is difficult, though here again, it is possible to point to certain fundamental needs. In Chapter II and again in Chapter V we drew attention to the necessity which sooner or later arises for an interpretation of life. The main psychological conditions for the emergence of this need seem to be the maturation of the intellectual grasp to the level at which abstract phrases and concepts can be understood; and an emotional development to the point at which questions of personal survival after death arise. If we are honest in our teaching, whilst we shall recognize the need of the adolescent for reaching an interpretation of

> the heavy and the weary weight
> Of all this unintelligible world,

we shall not seek to impose by influence or prestige any one interpretation—religious, ethical, scientific, or philosophic. Adults should not shrink from a statement of personal convictions; but they should be prepared to state also the grounds on which they are held, to leave the way open to other conceptions, and to present fairly the varying viewpoints of mankind. Corporate worship of an inspirational rather than religious kind, unwedded to dogma or theology and satisfying fundamental emotional and aesthetic needs, is an excellent start and finish to the school day. Moral and spiritual purpose unobtrusively a part of each item in the curriculum, examples of plain living and high thinking, and fine and genuine ideals in life and in literature, will do more to stabilize the spiritual development of boys and girls than official piety and enforced attendance at religious services.

None of these things—the Humanities, Science, Technical or

Commercial education—is, *ipso facto*, either 'cultural' or 'utilitarian'. Nor are the conceptions which underlie these two words necessarily antithetic. Nothing could be more grimly utilitarian than a 'set book' mugged up to pass an examination! All rests with the teacher and with a firm grasp of the fact that, certainly until sixteen, harmonious mental, emotional and physical development within the bounds of individual potentialities is the objective of education. Bodies of knowledge, training, skills, are only means to the attainment of that end.

Individual and Group Methods. Remembering the range of individual variation, we see that the needs of each child are differently balanced; and less than at any other time can youths be fitted to a mass advance. Increasingly, therefore, the teens should see an expansion in all directions, of opportunities to proceed at one's own pace and to follow individual lines of development. This is not to advocate a rampant individualism but rather a diversity within the unity of the group. The increased gregariousness of the period and the growing interest in social activities may become the basis of deliberate training for life in a community. Group activities provide opportunities for emotional education in the art of tolerating another's viewpoint, of exchanging opinions without heat, of subduing personal aims to corporate needs, of co-operation to a common end, and of accepting responsibility for others. It is in such activities that citizens are born, not in formal lessons on civics. By providing differing kinds of community, the home, the school, and the club can all contribute in complementary fashion to development and in their several ways build up habitual modes of behaviour to meet the multiplex demands of adult life.

Co-education. Each in its way, too, may further the sex training of the adolescent which is the core of emotional education and not a matter of biology only. Knowledge of facts unemotionally imparted is important but by itself insufficient. For

right development boys and girls need to acquire an unsenti-
mental approach to each other, the ability to work and play
together as a matter of course. Such an adjustment is unlikely
where segregation is strictly enforced in the teens, as it is for
example in single-sex boarding-schools.

Co-education presents some difficulties. It has been argued
that there is a natural tendency sanctioned in some (but by no
means all) primitive societies for the sexes to draw apart at or
just after puberty and that familiarity with the opposite sex
breeds contempt. More serious is the contention that there
are a number of sex differences in ability, rate of maturation,
and interests which make a common educational provision
impossible.

In a recent research, Moreton[1] cites the replies of experienced
headmasters of co-educational schools, some of whom agree
that there is a tendency for boys and girls in some cases to draw
apart, an observation confirmed by common experience. But
equally frequent are periods of flirtation, shy approach, and so
on. For none of these can precise age limits be fixed, and the
phases may alternate in the same individual or group. Practi-
cally, these tendencies do not present a serious difficulty, since
boys and girls may be allowed, if they wish, to separate out for
a time in class and in social activities; and sex rivalries, tactfully
handled and played down, do not reach serious proportions.
The suggestion that familiarity breeds contempt scarcely bears
scrutiny. There is no evidence that scholars from co-educational
schools marry less frequently or less happily than those from
single-sex schools. Of men and women questioned by Moreton,
156 found co-education helpful in regard to the relationships
with the opposite sex as against 10 who found it harmful;
103 found single-sex education harmful against only 11 who
found it helpful.

[1] 'Attitudes of Teachers and Scholars towards Co-education', *B. Journ. Ed. P.*,
vol. xvi, pt. 2, 1946. See also Valentine, contribution to the *Year Book of Education*,
1936, p. 322; and Howard, *The Mixed School* (London, 1928).

Sex Differences. Physical differences between the sexes are of course marked and increasingly apparent as adolescence proceeds. This means that for games, physical training and the like, some measure of segregation is desirable though, in the later teens, perhaps even this is not invariably or entirely necessary, provided that boys and girls are not pitted against each other. Differences in innate intelligence and in special abilities are not equally well established. There is some support for the suggestion that boys and men are more variable—that is, that there are more highly intelligent and more subnormal boys and men than women and girls—but none for an average superiority in intelligence in either sex. Girls as a whole appear to succeed better in verbal, boys in mathematical and mechanical, subjects, though it is probable that factors of culture and environment have a bearing here. Furthermore the differences in these respects within each sex group, are greater than any to be observed between the sexes.

The one mental difference which seems to be clearly established is that referred to in Chapter IV—the tendency for the aggressive impulses to predominate in the boy and the inhibitive in the girl. Here again the range of individual differences within each sex is great, and segregation, whilst it might reduce the variability of a group, would not by any means abolish it. The aggressiveness of the male to some extent accounts for the boy's greater readiness to experiment and bolder approach to fresh problems. The girl is more apt to be timid and over-conscientious. Where boys and girls are educated together, these differences, skilfully handled, may contribute to the development of each. The girl may learn an experimental boldness and the boy something of conscientious industry.

Differences in the age of onset of puberty and of the consequent emotional developments are more difficult to meet; but it is a difficulty primarily of educating adolescents and pre-adolescents together—a difficulty that must arise in the teens,

II

though less acutely, in single-sex schools. The practical solution is not segregation of the sexes: it is that from the age of eleven onwards there should be an increasing use of individual methods designed to meet the needs and interests of each child and not a rough Procrustean forcing of all to conform and progress evenly together.

Independence. Co-education will provide a suitable background against which the emotional training of the adolescent can proceed. It is essential also to provide outlets for other powerful drives manifesting themselves in the teens. The increased aggressiveness of both sexes, the desire to find a self and to achieve independence, need recognition and careful social training. The authoritarian discipline which is accepted in middle childhood breeds resentment, particularly in the adolescent boy. By degrees, independence in choice of studies and in the disposal of leisure time should be conceded. So too the boy and girl should be given increasing responsibility for property, for money, and for the well-being of others. School societies with elected representatives whose authority is respected by the school as a whole, co-operative projects, debating societies, school camps, games, and so on, all provide a framework within which the adolescent can try out powers of leadership and self-discipline. None of these measures is likely to be successful if it is carried out without conviction on the part of the teachers. The responsibility and the power conceded must be real. The aim of the teacher should be steadily and by degrees to relinquish the complete control which he or she may accept in childhood, and to substitute for it the position of elder adviser whose advice is accepted or rejected on its merits alone.

Such a programme of training has to be carefully planned and applied consistently; and it must be nicely matched to the temperaments and capacities of the adolescents. Too much liberty and too many cares of office produce anxiety and the desire to be free of the burden; too little accords ill with growing independence. Adolescents should be allowed to feel 'the weight of chance desires', to experiment and fail, to experiment and succeed. School, club, and home should provide, as well as a microcosm of the striving world, 'a mild and pleasant rest named Beulah', a place of refuge from the 'long wing'd arrows of thought'.

Discipline. The way to self-discipline is easy neither for the adolescent nor for those who have to deal with him. This is especially true with most children who have been educated in schools under an arbitrary discipline. There will be occasions when the categoric 'thou shalt' or 'thou shalt not' enforced by power would be a relief and short cut. The young people themselves may even complain, as one group did to the writer[1] that 'you are not strict enough with us'. Interventions by adult authority cannot always be entirely avoided; they should however become less and less frequent; and should be only a last resort when the individual needs a firm direction or the public opinion of the group claims it as inevitable.

Discipline has its positive side. The success of the pre-service training units during the recent war must be attributed to the clear way in which they canalized the needs of the adult community for the service and loyalty of youth. The motive was real and urgent. The training given looked forward to a tangible future. Unless education can find a similarly real and compelling motive of self-dedication, the fierce desire of the adolescent to count in the scheme of things will be exploited to perverse ends as it was in the Nazi Youth Movement. Projects of reconstruction and schemes of social betterment offer scope for idealism, room even for a temporary fanaticism, which proves for a season that the 'tigers of wrath are wiser than the horses of instruction'. Tolerance is not built from lukewarm enthusiasms and cold water cast upon the hot partisanship of youth; it is as natural for youth to embrace revolution as it is for age to prefer

[1] And to Kitchen (op. cit.).

the *status quo*. One thing is certain: without a good cause to fight for, boys and girls will either embrace a bad one or sink into emotional apathy and feeble cynicism.

III. THE EMOTIONALLY DISTURBED AND EDUCATIONALLY RETARDED

We may hope that as education is based more and more on the emotional needs of growing youth, and as we come to know more clearly the correct critical periods for introducing this or that educational technique or field of knowledge, backwardness will be confined to those of lower than average intelligence and that even these will be taught to make the most of their limited talent. In the next few years however, as the facts presented at the beginning of this chapter suggest, the teacher in the Youth College or Secondary Modern School will be faced with the urgent tasks of remedying educational defect, restoring educational morale, and removing or lessening the emotional difficulties which, whether as cause or effect, lie behind these.

Special Difficulties. All three are closely interrelated and cannot be solved in isolation. Problem adolescents are likely to have built up evasive techniques over nine or ten years, which, having become habitual, are not readily abandoned. The increased self-consciousness of the period too adds a sting of humiliation to feelings of inferiority. More critical than ever before of their own lame efforts, backward boys and girls are apt to pursue forms of self-assertion more apparently profitable than application to a thankless task: they prefer the leadership of a band of malcontents, or indulgence in petulant and self-exculpatory criticism of teachers, or trouble-making of the kind which does not call for extreme methods but which is irritating and disturbing to others. More likely to escape notice, but no less seriously in need of aid, are those who prefer, by quiescence and apathy, to be adjudged lazy rather than backward.

Little progress will be made with such cases until their

emotional difficulties are solved and until the self-distrust and sense of inferiority in the use of the simplest intellectual tools are exorcized. A clear and genuine purposefulness in the curriculum, a close and apparent relation of the effort demanded to goals which the boy or girl can see as worth attaining, are more than ever necessary, though, alone, likely to be insufficient. The whole outlook of the adolescent on the self and on life must be re-educated. Within this rubric, there is no one right and universally successful method. With some, a waiting policy is best, a deliberate willingness to give them their heads in the early teens and then to seize the opportunity presented by the calmer period of late adolescence. With others, tactful reassurance and praise will do much. Careful manipulation of learning situations so that success is achieved fairly easily in the early stages, a progressive restoration of morale, the avoidance of competition with others, the keeping of a personal (and private) chart of progress, a positive attitude on the part of the teacher which allows no doubt of ultimate success, and an inconspicuous readiness to help at the point where unaided efforts cannot achieve success, are useful methods. The emphasis should be on individual goals and on individual standards, on assignments of work suited to the capacity of John or Mary and not to fifteen-year-olds as an average group.

Group Methods. Group methods too can have great value with disturbed adolescents. Discussion carried on with numbers just large enough to give a certain amount of impersonality to what is said and yet small enough to remain intimate (not less than four or five and not more than ten or twelve) can be made to serve a therapeutic purpose. The teacher should enter merely as an older member, though he or she may steer the conversation tactfully into personal channels, without however making direct personal reference inevitable, or giving the idea that anyone is being 'got at'. By such means, many adolescent preoccupations and sources of conflict can be brought out into the open without alarming self-consciousness or provoking a defensive reticence. Practical questions such as the use of cosmetics, flirtations, losing one's temper, attitudes to parents, dancing, pocket-money, conditions at the office or factory, what is the use of learning this, that, or the other, clashes of temperament, self-discipline, worth-while aims and ideals, and so on can all be fruitfully discussed. The watchful leader in such a group will be swift to seize upon the opportunity (without preaching, for that would be fatal) of decreasing the sense of lonely struggle which perplexes so many boys and girls, of giving reassurance here and counteracting cynicism there. To do this requires a background of knowledge of the questions which vex the adolescent mind and of the particular personalities who form the group in question. The results will not be immediately apparent: though a shrewd observer may from time to time notice the unexpected smile when an apparently casual word strikes home and makes a rough place smooth.

In the early teens such methods are more likely to be successful with girls than with boys, because of their greater preoccupation with personal problems and their earlier emotional maturity. With boys, straight friendly talks that are short and apparently arise by chance are an effective alternative.

Such remedial methods are after all merely an intensification of what is necessary in the education of all adolescents. It cannot be too often reiterated that, even more than the child, the youth must be studied as an individual. This is only in-directly a plea for small classes in the secondary stage. Small groups are an undeniable advantage in some directions, and especially in that they make it possible for the teacher to study each individual intensively. But even with groups of more than thirty, the devising of individual schemes of work is not impossible; it is in fact more than ever necessary.

The Role of Adults. One thing remains to be said explicitly though it has been hinted at before. All-important to the adolescent are the adults with whom he or she comes into contact. The reality which must dominate the curriculum should be apparent in them too. Sincerity, conviction, enthusiasm, are of incalculable importance. Men and women who have thought out for themselves a clear set of values and are willing to state and defend them without dogmatism, who teach what they believe in and only what they believe in, who are prepared to meet confidence with confidence, to share doubts as well as certainties, will, no matter what their limitations in other respects, win the affection and interest of adolescents. One is tempted to say that it matters little what is taught, but that it does matter greatly who teaches it. Without a genuine liking for those who teach them the boy or girl may learn to transfer their indifference or dislike of the person to just those values which he represents. More even than the child, the youth needs someone to soften the sting of failure by a kindly word and stamp in the lessons of success by skilful analysis, someone to relieve the strain when life is proving too exacting or destructive impulses are getting the upper hand.

The well-adjusted man or woman can make a great contribution to the emotional development of the adolescent by acting as a reference point, an

ever fixed mark
That looks on tempests and is never shaken.

It is perhaps difficult at times to realize that the self-confident, conceited, aggressively poised youth is craving for a clear expression of love from an admired adult; or that the irritating abberations of behaviour, the noisy showing off, the boisterous vivacity or melancholy surliness, are directed to the same end. The teacher or the youth leader, the friendly aunt or uncle, are free of involvement in the past emotional development of the boy or girl in a way that no parent can ever be. They are thus excellently placed to supply the adolescent need for acceptance and for affection. Anyone who cannot find it in his heart to give this to the half-formed youths in front of him, who cannot share, at least in retrospect, the crusading idealism of the teens, the burning interests, the flashing hope, the bleak despair, and all the thousand poignancies of the period, had better sell iron-mongery or stocks and shares—do anything other than enter a club or a school.

CHAPTER VII

ALL THE WORLD BEFORE THEM

I. PROBLEMS AND PRINCIPLES OF VOCATIONAL GUIDANCE

The Importance of a Job. To most adolescents, work is a part
of the adult social pattern to which they long to conform; and
initial success or failure in finding a job not infrequently becomes
highly significant in the finding of a self as an indication of the
power to achieve independence. A job is an index of worth-
whileness, of the community's need for the efforts of the
individual, and a necessary prelude to the achievement of self-
support. The extra pocket-money which earning provides is a
factor in the maintenance of friendships, and the pursuit of
interests. To the girl, earning represents often the first step
towards emancipation from the home, the ability to buy smarter
clothes and beauty preparations. To the boy, it gives the power
to stand treats; and, at a later stage, earning capacity is an
important part of sexual prestige and attractiveness, and provides
the necessary economic basis for marriage. Hence it is to be
expected that irregular or casual employment in the teens, or,
what is worse, unemployment, should produce a feeling of
apathy, a complete loss of a sense of the value of time, and a
feeling of 'It's like as if you were dead'.[1]

Among boys especially the thought of a vocation becomes
the focus for many fears and anxieties as well as hopes and
ambitions. The girl who lays long-term plans for a career is

[1] Lush, *The Young Adult in South Wales,* p. 42 (Cardiff, 1941); *Men Without
Work,* Pilgrim Trust, especially pp. 128, 151(Cambridge, 1938).

perhaps the exception; but the most thoughtless of boys is inclined to look into the future, though he may not do so far enough or on a very well-informed basis. For both sexes, the first job is an initiation into the adult world, and is looked forward to as bringing with it a substantial instalment of the privileges of maturity. It is the subject of endless day-dreams and reveries, many of them fantastically divorced from the reality which eventually meets the young person. The world of office, factory, or shop is, during the hours of work, a more regimented one than that of home and school. But the luncheon break, and spare moments at the beginning and ending of the day, may be an abrupt initiation into life. The whole psychological atmosphere is different; home and school, whatever their shortcomings, usually have the interests of the young person as one of their principal objectives: he or she is of importance, as a rounded personality. In the earning world only one aspect of the self is of critical importance, it seems—one's ability to do the job; and where the adolescent is working as a youth among adults, the sense of loneliness and of impersonal forces in the environment may be overwhelming.[1]

The effect of the sudden change from school to work is often salutary, bringing a rapid maturation in outlook, tastes, habits, and behaviour; and as James and Moore have shown,[2] even profoundly affecting the use made of leisure time. Where the adolescent is under good supervision which continues to put the needs of the developing personality first, this critical period may be of the utmost value. One of the advantages of the old system of apprenticeship was the stress it laid on the responsibility of the employer, not merely for the technical training of his apprentice, but for his moral and social development as well. The modern employer who accepts such a responsibility is the

[1] A vivid account of the experience of one adolescent is given by W. Kenworthy in 'The First Years at Work', *Human Factor*, vol. ix, No. 9, 1935.

[2] 'Adolescent Leisure in a Working-Class District', *Occ. Psych.*, vol. xiv, 1940; vol. xviii, pts. 1 and 2, 1944.

exception. More often than not, the fourteen-year-old has been thrown among adults who know little of his needs and has had no one from whom advice or guidance could be sought. The results are familiar: an increased instability and cynicism, an exaggerated sense of the gulf which separates employer and employed, and a swift adoption of the attitude that work itself is something barely to be tolerated.

Blind Alley Employment. Much of this friction, so damaging to the right growth of character, can be traced to the conditions which beset the first four or so years of the earning life of the average child. Pre-war surveys in Liverpool[1] showed that nearly half the boys leaving school at fourteen entered 'blind-alley' occupations as van-boys, shop-boys, billiard markers, errand-boys, and so on; and another quarter were unemployed. As the occupational grade of the father declined, the percentage of boys and girls entering blind-alley jobs rose —two-thirds of the sons and more than two-thirds of the daughters of fathers who were unskilled manual workers entered posts as shop-boys, factory hands, messengers, and similar occupations which held out no future prospects of employment. The proportions of those who found themselves in 'progressive' jobs increased throughout the teens until, in the 18–21 age-groups 70 per cent. of boys and 62·4 per cent. of girls were in some kind of work 'suitable for adults' and of a more or less progressive nature. But even at that age, 18·6 per cent. of boys and 10·2 per cent. of girls were unemployed, and 10 per cent. of the boys and a quarter of the girls still lingered on in tasks that could lead them nowhere.

The instability of adolescent employment is reflected in figures of labour turn-over—the number of those leaving in one year expressed as a percentage of the number employed. In her inquiry into Labour Turnover in Leeds, Mrs. Raphael[2]

[1] Caradog Jones, etc., *Social Survey of Merseyside*, vol. iii, ch. vii (London, 1934).
[2] 'An Enquiry into Labour Turnover in the Leeds District', *Occ. Psych.*, vol. xii, No. 4, 1938.

found that whereas for men aged eighteen and over the figure was 9 per cent., for boys it was 26 per cent.; the corresponding figure for women was 30 per cent. and for girls 48 per cent. An analysis of the reasons given for leaving showed that 65 per cent. of boys and 76 per cent. of girls left their jobs because of difficulties which could have been avoided—temporary dissatisfactions and disharmonies, misunderstandings, and the like.

Vocational Maladjustment. Figures however do not fully reveal the heavy toll of vocational maladjustment in adolescence. The dull youth labouring at a job beyond his capacity may scrape through without frequent or glaring mistakes; but constant anxiety or a feeling of inadequacy may lead him to seek compensation in skylarking or even delinquency.[1] The brighter boy or girl whose talents and capacities are not called out by a routine repetitive task perhaps takes refuge in day-dreams, or vague discontent. Lack of satisfaction, anxiety, overstrain, under-employment, a job which makes physical demands which the organism cannot easily meet—all these are sources of unrest. In extreme cases they lead to a physical or mental breakdown, and in less extreme cases to fatigue, irritability, instability of employment, and failure to adjust to others at work or at home. This is a drain on human happiness and efficiency that we can ill afford.[2]

The present conditions of acute labour shortage, the operation of the Essential Work Order, and the higher wages paid to juveniles in industry, probably mask some of this wastage. The activities of enlightened employers and of experienced juvenile employment officers are doing something to lessen the dissatisfactions and disillusionments with which many children meet in

---

[1] A discussion of the possibilities of satisfactory compensation will be found in Alec Rodger, 'How People Compensate or Adjust Themselves for Lack of Ability', *Human Factor*, vol. xi, No. 11, 1937.

[2] Smith, *Introduction to Industrial Psychology*; Culpin and Smith, *The Nervous Temperament in Industry*, I.H.R.B. Pamphlet No. 61, 1930; Smith, Culpin and Farmer, *A Study of Telegraphists' Cramp*, I.H.R.B. Pamphlet No. 43, 1927.

the first years of their industrial life. Neither however can do more than mitigate the problem of the boy or girl who is vocationally maladjusted, or who by the age of eighteen or nineteen has held a variety of insignificant posts without at the same time acquiring a background of skill and experience which is an industrial asset.

Vocational Interests. Some of the difficulty may be traced to the instability of the interests of adolescents themselves and to their ignorance of the vocational field. Lehman and Witty,[1] studying nearly 27,000 American boys and girls between the ages of eight and eighteen, are forced to the conclusion that no phase of human nature is subject to such marked change as that reflected in the expressed vocational interests and preferences of adolescents. Fryer[2] found only a slight relationship between vocational ambitions and vocational potentiality and between interest and proficiency. Freeston[3] in her two surveys of the vocational interests of elementary-school children in this country, in 1938 and 1944, found considerable evidence of conflict between more or less incompatible vocational aims in boys and girls, increasing, especially in the latter, in the critical years from eleven to fourteen. Further, the proportions of her groups who made 'possible' choices declined between the ages of eight and fourteen. The reasons prompting even suitable choices were far from logical in more than half the cases even at thirteen or fourteen, though there was some evidence to show that better reasons are assigned with increasing age. Her later survey suggests that the closer contact between the child and the adult world brought about by the war has had the effect of introducing

---

[1] 'One More Study of the Permanence of Interests', *Journ. Ed. Psych.*, vol. xxii, No. 7, 1931.
[2] 'Predicting Abilities from Interests', *Journ. App. Psych.*, vol. ix, 1927; 'The Significance of Interests for Vocational Prognosis', *Ment. Hygiene*, vol. xiii, No. 2, 1924.
[3] 'The Vocational Interests of Elementary School Children', *Occ. Psych.*, vol. xiii, No. 3, 1939; 'The Influence of the War on Juvenile and Adolescent Vocational Interests', *Occ. Psych.*, vol. xx, No. 3, 1936.

a greater realism into their vocational outlook. In 1938 most of the girls depicted themselves inside the home although most of them would have to do some kind of industrial work. In 1944 many more showed themselves in industry. There is still evidence of conflicting aims, but it is diminished; and a far higher proportion make choices which it might be possible for them to achieve.

In secondary-school groups the position seems to be no better. Lingwood[1] found that only 26 per cent. of her secondary-school girls possessed good, correct information about the vocation of their choice, and then only about careers such as teaching with which they had had direct contact.

Valentine and Ritchie in 1927,[2] studying the reasons given by secondary-school boys for their choice of occupation, found that 34 per cent. of the reasons alleged were trivial or irrelevant —the mere ease with which a job could be obtained, or prejudice against manual work, and preference for a clean job. 32 per cent. gave as a reason their liking for a particular school subject; another 15 per cent. show 'gleams of the hopes and enthusiasms of youth', natural at that age but dangerous lest a wave of emotion should carry a youth into waters beyond his depth.

Among the examples cited are some which would be laughable were the ignorance they indicate not so serious. 'The profession that I have chosen,' writes one boy, 'is that of a lawyer. My reasons are that I have the gift of being a good talker and linguist. . . . What influenced me was how I got out of scrapes at school or at home with ease by using my tongue and not necessarily telling lies about it.' Another writes 'a prominent phrenologist said I was suited as an organizer or buyer, and would be very good at figures.' Even, it seems, among those who are considering teaching, about which they should know

[1] 'The Vocational Information Possessed by Secondary School Girls', *Occ. Psych.*, vol. xv, No. 4, 1941.
[2] 'An Enquiry as to the Reasons for the Choice of Occupations among Secondary School Pupils', *Forum of Ed.*, vol. v, No. 2, 1927.

something definite, though the proportions of satisfactory responses given increase with age from eleven to seventeen, there are never more than 45 per cent. who give good or satisfactory reasons.[1] In another inquiry by Valentine,[2] this time with university graduates who had already committed themselves to the teaching profession, 26 per cent. of men and 17 per cent. of women adduced 'inability to change', 'no alternative prospect', and 'stopgap' as among their principal reasons for entering the profession. He concludes that about one-third of the men students and one-fourth of the women give, as their *main* reason for entering teaching, some unworthy motive. In this unreliability and inadequacy of the motives which too often prompt an occupational choice lies a fruitful source of unhappiness, maladjustment, and inefficiency later.

The reasons given for his vocational choice by an adolescent may be adequate, and entry to the job possible for a child of his background and ability; yet his ambition may be totally unrelated to the conditions of the labour market. We have seen this occur in the 1930's with teaching and other professions. Pallister's research with Dundee school-leavers shows that it is potentially a serious cause of friction in a humbler sphere.[3] 30 per cent. of girls wished to become shop assistants, 27 per cent. to enter factories, and 20 per cent. offices—a balance quite out of proportion to the needs of the area. Over half the boys wished to enter a skilled trade, whereas in the previous year only 10 per cent. of leavers undertook the necessary apprenticeship. Many boys expressed preferences for occupations in which there were few openings and wished to enter them without adequate preparation. Similar results have been obtained by

[1] Austin, 'An Analysis of the Motives of Adolescents for the Choice of the Teaching Profession,' B. Journ. Ed. P., vol. i, pt. 1, 1931.
[2] 'An Enquiry as to the Reasons for the Choice of the Teaching Profession by University Students', B. Journ. Ed. P., vol. iv, pt. 3, November 1934.
[3] 'The Vocational Preferences of School Leavers in a Scottish Industrial Area' B. Journ. P., vol. xxix, pt. 2, 1938.

investigators studying American youth.[1]   From whatever cause, it appears that schools have not led their pupils either to appraise carefully their own potentialities or to survey realistically the opportunities which exist in the world of occupations.

The Psychological Background of Interests.   The expressed interests and ambitions of the adolescent, then, though they should not be ignored, must be examined with caution before being made the basis of a vocational choice. We must consider the part they are playing in the psychic life of the boy or girl. An interest may be the genuine outcome of talent in a particular direction and thus of great and direct significance. On the other hand, environmental influences—as for instance an artistic or musical family—may stimulate an enthusiasm which rests on no outstanding capacity. Dangerous to future adjustment (and peculiarly liable at adolescence) are compensatory interests— choices of study or vocation which are determined by marked personality difficulties—the repressed solitary child who desires 'work with animals', the boy or girl who, failing to achieve success in ordinary school work, studies a comparatively obscure field, Egyptology, ethnology, or the like, to cut a dash intel- lectually; the unbalanced youth who seeks in psychology the solution of his own conflicts and crises; the diffident, shy girl who wants to go on the stage; the boy in revolt against conven- tion and his parents, who at an early age embraces revolutionary politics.[2]

Allied or at variance with these main trends are other drives operating in the personality. The desire to be like the rest of one's group is with many a powerful determinant of choice— and not necessarily a right one. Berdie[3] studying university students found that 73 per cent. of sons of skilled tradesmen had

---

[1] Roeber and Garfield, 'A Study of the Occupational Interests of High School Pupils in Terms of Grade Placements', *Journ. Ed. Psych.*, vol. xxxiv, No. 6, 1941.
[2] Davies, 'The Place of Interests in Vocational Adjustment', *Occ. Psych.*, vol. xiii, No. 1, 1939.
[3] 'Factors Associated with Vocational Interests', *Journ. Ed. Psych.*, vol. xxxiv, No. 5, 1943.

primary or secondary patterns of interests in the skilled trade group; whereas 63 per cent. of the sons of business executives wished to enter business. Such results show the influence of the home environment; but the desire to conform may operate in more subtle ways. It may determine the choice of an occupation, intrinsically unsuitable, just because most of one's friends and relatives have work of a similar kind, or it may prevent one from accepting a job which is at all unusual by the standards of one's group. A desire for security similarly operates strongly with some, particularly with those who come from families in which the maintenance of economic independence has been a source of anxiety. Drives towards activity and work, the full employment of one's energies and abilities, towards self-assertion—either by excelling others, by belonging to a superior social group, by the exercise of power, or by self-display—may all enter.[1] Somewhat later in development, and especially powerful with the gifted, altruism, protective impulses, humanitarianism, and the like, may determine the choice of a career of service to others through nursing or social work.

There is another aspect of interests which is of fundamental importance to future adjustment in a job. Though the expression which they seek may vary, and although any of the psychological factors we have been discussing may underlie and modify them, it is possible to assign roughly the individual's pattern of interests to one of three major groups.[2] There are those children who, from early years, are interested predominantly in what might be called intellectual activities—books, ideas, culture, theoretical considerations, and the like. There are others whose chosen activities are markedly practical, constructional, and manipulative, or who prefer occupations demanding physical expression. There is a third group who prefer activities which

[1] M. D. Vernon, 'The Relationship of Occupation to Personality', *B.Journ.P.*, vol. xxxi, pt. 4, 1942; 'Characteristic Motivation in the Activities of School Girls', ibid., vol. xxix, pt. 3, 1939.
[2] Davies, paper cited above.

would be described as social; they like working with people rather than with things, they enjoy gossiping, organizing and directing the activities of others, and so on. These classifications are empirical and far from being hard and fast distinctions. But, by a longitudinal study of the child, it is possible to see in which field his or her activities have principally lain, though it is very important to remember that adolescence may bring about profound modifications in the direction of interests and that interests in the intellectual and social fields are not likely to declare themselves decisively until a comparatively late stage in development.

Sex Differences. In the presence or absence of such drives as we have been considering and their effects, there are marked sex differences, some of them culturally and environmentally determined, others of them innate. The vocational choices of girls, partly because of difficulties in the occupational field itself, tend to be more restricted than those of boys. English and American researches agree that teaching, nursing and office work, semi-skilled factory work, domestic work, and shop assistant cover the ambitions of most ordinary girls. Among boys the choice open is wider, but engineering, office work, semi-scientific work like 'chemist', teaching, and draughtsmanship, attract them most, though carpentry and farming have a considerable following. The motives adduced show interesting variation. In one large inquiry 'like it' is the most frequent reason given by girls and boys; 'money' is second for boys, 'fitted for it' second for girls and third for boys, and third for girls are various altruistic reasons.[1]

The vocational choice of the girl is influenced by the prospect of marriage. Not a few employers are unwilling to train a girl who may leave them before her usefulness repays her training; parents too are more reluctant to pay for extended education for

[1] Hurlock and Jansing, 'The Vocational Attitudes of Boys and Girls of High School Age', *Journ. Gen. Psych,* vol. xliv, pt. 1, 1934.

their daughters than for their sons. Even among girls of high ability, marriage is felt as a bar to the continuance of a career by all except rather more than one-fifth,[1] and among girls of more ordinary calibre the proportion would probably be higher, though many for economic reasons might later continue at work.

That marriage for many girls will conflict with a career may account for the difference in the vocational outlook of the sexes. Compared with boys, girls have as a rule less knowledge of possibilities and of what is involved in a proposed career; they tend to take a more 'horizontal' view, looking rather at the level they wish to be on than at the ladder they have to climb, are more interested in emotional satisfaction, and less in financial reward, security, or prospects of advancement: they are less ready to accept the implications of their own limitations, and more inclined to indulge in the pseudo ambition of the day-dream.[2]

Vocational Information. The foregoing analysis is sufficient to indicate something of the difficulties which beset the entry of the adolescent into the industrial world; and something of the haphazard, ill-informed motives which prompt so many unsuitable choices. There is reason to believe that after the age of sixteen, interests achieve more stability, that the adolescent knows a little more about the occupational field and is more likely to make an adjustment to a suitable job. Thus the raising of the school-leaving age will do something, by the delay it imposes, to make vocational choice a little more likely to be successful. The indications are that of those who formulate a clear ambition, most do so between fifteen and seventeen, though other factors, such as prolonged education or immaturity, may operate to delay a decision; and there may be a considerable time lag

[1] Mercer, 'Some Occupational Attitudes of Girls', *Occ. Psych.*, vol. xiv, No. 1, 1940.
[2] Stott, 'Some Differences between Boys and Girls in Vocational Guidance', *Occ. Psych.*, vol. xix, No. 3, 1945.

between the appearance of a vocational interest and its acceptance as the basis of a life's work.[1]

Without adequate vocational information in their possession, however, boys and girls will still be liable to mistaken choices. Comprehensive information on careers entering, as an integral part of the curriculum, into the studies of adolescents has already been advocated. As a study of the 'work, health, and happiness of mankind', it need be no less 'cultural' than ancient history; of no less 'disciplinary' value than geometry or translation into Latin prose. It has the merit, especially for the boy or girl of average intelligence, of direct and obvious connection with life in the world beyond the walls of their school. Begun as a combined history and geography or 'English studies' course in the very early teens, it can be broadened into a survey of the whole field of work, of its organization and integration, of the economic forces which lie behind it, of the raw materials on which it depends, and of the markets in which its products are sold. As a part of such a course of study, particularly as the time of school-leaving approaches, careful examination can be made of particular fields of occupation, specific trades and industries. Such an approach should be supplemented by visits to factories, offices, shops, and by well-informed but unbiased talks by outsiders—men and women actually doing the jobs of which they speak. The information given needs to be detailed and accurate but free from 'inspirational' persuasion; and it should cover the widest possible field, laying stress not merely upon rewards, but also upon the demands of particular vocations.

The need for this dissemination of information about careers is being realized. Many schools, especially of the grammar-school type, have done something to lay before their pupils the requirements of a range of occupations. Such information will stimulate inquiry, enlarge the scope of ambition, and give a clearer insight into the requirements of various jobs. It will not

[1] Kaplan, 'Age and Vocational Choice', *Journ. Gen. Psych.*, vol. lxviii, pt. 1, 1946.

by itself ensure that John or Mary formulates a clear and practicable plan of action likely to lead to lifelong satisfaction with
his or her chosen career. Vocational adjustment depends, as the
work of numerous industrial psychologists has clearly established, upon a matching of the powers and qualities of the
person to the demands of an occupation. In this matter our
information is far from complete and precise, but we do know
enough to prevent wild and tragic errors being made.

For a wide range of jobs, maximum and minimum levels of
intelligence have been determined, outside which success is less
likely. This is perhaps most clearly seen in the case of the
professions, in which no one is likely to do well without high
enough ability; but it is equally true in another direction, as for
example when the highly intelligent girl, who might have become
a doctor or lawyer, quickly finds chocolate-packing or copy-
typing intolerably boring. The actual range of ability in any
occupation from highest to lowest is fairly great, and the overlap
between occupations near together on the scale considerable.
Nevertheless from the general level of intelligence of a boy or
girl it is possible to suggest one field of occupations in which
success is more likely than in others. Table VI[1] shows roughly
the levels of the various occupational grades.

Aptitudes. In many occupations, while a minimum level of
general ability is an essential, success depends as much upon the
possession of special capacities of the type we discussed in
Chapter V. For example, while a good general education and
considerable intelligence are necessary, the youth whose verbal
aptitude is low is not likely to do well as a newspaper reporter
or as a salesman. Similarly a high degree of manual dexterity
and mechanical aptitude are essential to many engineering jobs

---

[1] This table is based upon that given in Burt et al., *A Study in Vocational Guidance*,
I.H.R.B. Pamphlet No. 33, 1926. It is reproduced by permission of the Con-
troller of H.M. Stationery Office. See also Cattell, 'Occupational Norms of
Intelligence and Standardisation of an Adult Intelligence Test', *B. Journ. P.*, vol.
xxv, pt. 1, for a substantially similar table.

TABLE VI

CLASSIFICATION OF VOCATIONS ACCORDING TO DEGREE OF INTELLIGENCE REQUIRED

	I.Q.[1]	Description	Type of Work
Class I	Over 150 Per cent. of adult male population = 0·1	Higher Professional and Administrative	Lawyer, physician, teacher (university and grammar), author, editor, scientist, artist, managing director, civil service clerk (Cl. I), company secretary, broker, chartered accountant, architect, analytical chemist, professional engineer.
Class II	130–150 Per cent. of adult male population = 3·0	Lower Professional, Technical and Executive	Teacher (primary), civil service clerk (Cl. II), accountant, secretary, executive clerk, dentist, veterinary surgeon, reporter, social worker, factory superintendent, surveyor, merchant, auctioneer, buyer, commercial traveller, technical engineer, designer.
Class III	115–130 Per cent. of adult male population = 12·0	Clerical and highly skilled work	Shorthand-typist, book-keeper, bank or office clerk, wholesale salesman, musician, specialist teacher (gym, music, domestic science), small merchant, insurance agent, electrician, telegraphist, druggist, hospital nurse, compositor, engraver, lithographer, draughtsman, photographer, toolmaker, patternmaker, moulder, machine inspector, showroom assistant, foreman.

Class IV	100–115 Per cent. of adult male population=26·0	Skilled work	Tailor, dressmaker, milliner, upholsterer, engine, tram and bus driver, policeman, telephone operator, printer, mechanic, turner, fitter, miller, finisher, hand-riveter, cabinet maker, carpenter, plumber, blacksmith, mason, farmer, shop assistant, cashier, hairdresser, routine typist.
Class V	85–100 Per cent. of adult male population=33·0	Semi-skilled repetition work	Fairly mechanical repetition work requiring low degrees of skill, poorer commercial positions: barber, welder, tin and copper smith, driller, polisher, miner, furnace man, carter, bricklayer, painter, carpenter, baker, cook, shoemaker, textile worker, laundry worker, packer (delicate goods) postman, coachman, waiter or waitress, pageboy, domestic servant (better class).
Class VI	70–85 Per cent. of adult male population=19·0	Unskilled repetition work	Unskilled labour, coarse manual work, automatic machine worker, labourer, loader, navvy, fisherman, farmhand, groom, slater, chimney-sweep, packer, labeller, bottler, porter, messenger, deliverer, liftboy, and liftgirl, domestic servant (poorer class), factory workers generally.
Class VII	50–70 Per cent. of adult male population=7·0	Casual labour	Simplest routine work, and occasional employment on purely mechanical tasks under supervision.
Class VIII	Under 50 Per cent. of adult male population=0·2	Institutional	Unemployable (imbeciles and idiots).

[1] See page 92 for a discussion of the meaning of this term.

at the bench, whilst for other tasks—e.g. the *design* of mechanisms—number ability and mechanical aptitude must be combined with high intelligence and drawing ability. The girl whose manual dexterity and spatial perception are poor will not, probably, make a good dressmaker, whatever other qualities she may have. Even into comparatively humble tasks special capacities enter, and a job like the routine packing of chocolates or biscuits demands spatial perception and manual dexterity.

Physique. Many occupations make demands also on the physique. This is obvious in the case of tasks demanding physical strength or endurance—like labouring or navvying—or those which involve lifting, carrying, or pulling. Not perhaps so obvious are those which require strength of grip, steadiness and sureness of hand, ability to undergo the prolonged fatigue of standing or walking about. Certain fine machine operations (steadiness of hand, strength of grip) or the work of a bus conductor or a waitress might be cited as examples. Not unusually the physical demands are rather of the nature of contra-indications than positive requirements; flat feet should rule out a job requiring much walking; a tendency to rheumatism eliminates any task involving exposure to damp; colour-blindness an occupation such as engine-driver, decorator, or dress-designer; a disability like epilepsy or petit mal any work with dangerous machinery. Careful medical examination before taking up work, especially manual work, would do much to minimize the incidence of industrial disease and accidents. How essential it is, is shown by the fact that 19 per cent. of the children covered by Jewkes'[1] Lancashire survey were medically abnormal, and of over 500 children examined in a London vocational guidance experiment[2] more than *one-third* had one or more defects which ruled out certain kinds of employment.

Temperament. More subtle is the factor of temperamental

[1] *The Juvenile Labour Market* (London, 1938).
[2] Earle, *Methods of Choosing a Career*, p. 60 (London, 1931).

adjustment to a job and its conditions. For example, a girl the trend of whose interests has been towards working with people is more likely to find satisfaction in work like that of a sales-woman, involving contacts with her fellows, than in working alone handling stores; the boy whose chosen occupations have always lain among concrete objects will be happier handling bricks and mortar than in totting up figures. Those who delight in physical activity are not likely to be happy, or more than moderately successful, in a job that keeps them sitting still. On the other hand, those who are already introverted and prone to day-dreaming do not require a job which occupies the hand merely, leaving the mind free to brood. The child of engaging, sunny, co-operative disposition can use it as an asset in a job involving relationships with others; the born leader, ready to assume responsibility, can be given a job in which his or her self-confidence will become an advantage; the submissive and self-distrustful should avoid too heavy a demand upon their self-confidence, otherwise anxiety and breakdown may be the consequence. In this field the range and degree of variation seems unlimited, and the emotional and character developments of adolescence make assessment extremely difficult. Yet it is certainly possible by a study of the interests of the individual to assess whether they lie mainly in intellectual, concrete, or personal fields, to decide whether they are genuine and lasting, or whether they are compensatory and perhaps transitory. It is possible too to assess roughly the other temperamental charac-teristics and personality trends which are likely to be of impor-tance in finding a suitable life's work.

Personal Circumstances. There remain two other practical considerations of some importance. In capacity, physique, and temperament, one boy may be admirably fitted to become a lawyer or doctor; another might seem to be fit only for a semi-skilled task demanding neither great intelligence nor initiative. If however the first boy has had nothing but the rudiments of education and his parents cannot find the money for his training, then a career in the law or medicine is probably closed to him. If he attempts it, some such fate as that of Jude the Obscure may overtake him. The second boy may be the son of weathly parents, the traditions of whose family are against manual work; even if he takes to the bench he will find adjustment difficult because of the conflict between the two halves of his life. Cases like the first occur less frequently and less glaringly now than they used to and equality of opportunity in education should diminish them. Cases like the second produce the most difficult of all problems facing the vocational adviser, since questions of social prestige are so closely bound up with various occupations.

Plan of Attack. We may perhaps conveniently summarize this section by quoting the plan of attack for vocational guidance drawn up by the investigators of the National Institute of Industrial Psychology.[1] In order to assist any individual in making a right choice of occupation, we need to know:

1. His circumstances (financial, social, geographical, etc.).

2. His physical characteristics (especially disabilities of occupational significance, and such semi-physical characteristics as smartness of bearing, attractiveness of appearance, neatness of dress, and pleasantness of voice).

3. His attainments (particularly in work, games, and other leisure activities).

4. His general intelligence.

5. His special aptitudes (such as mechanical aptitude, manual dexterity, number aptitude, and aptitudes for drawing and music).

6. His interests (especially in intellectual activities, practical activities, and social activities).

7. His disposition (particularly as shown by his attitudes towards himself, towards others, and towards his work).

[1] Rodger, 'Planning for Vocational Guidance', *Occ. Psych.*, vol. xiii, No. 1, 1939.

Methods. Under some of these headings information is more easy to gather and more objective than under others. Personal circumstances can be gathered by interview and by home visits, and physical characteristics by a thorough medical examination. We have efficient tests of intelligence, both of the type which use words as their medium and of the kind in which ability is gauged through the handling of concrete material or diagrams and pictures. These tests, on which much research work has been carried out in recent years, are either of the pencil-and-paper type which can be given to large groups of boys and girls at once, or they consist of a number of small tests which have to be administered by a trained tester in a private interview. The former method means that up to a hundred or even more can be tested in an hour by a teacher with the minimum of special instruction in the method of procedure and the results can be marked by a clerk from a prepared key. This is obviously a great saving of time, an important factor in any comprehensive scheme of guidance. The individual tests have the merit of greater accuracy and of permitting the close study of a child. The procedure of administration, however, requires a trained psychologist and each case may take upwards of three-quarters of an hour. In practice it seems best to use the group tests of intelligence as a screen, and to supplement them in borderline cases by an individual examination.

In attempting to assess special abilities, we must distinguish between aptitude or capacity and attainment or skill. Aptitude refers to something inborn, a capacity which may or may not have been developed by education or training; attainment or skill is the result of innate qualities combined with experience, training, or education. For example, in a school in which the mathematics teaching is highly efficient, a boy of good intelligence and only moderate aptitude for number may manage to pass the School (or even Higher) Certificate mathematics with some success. If however he pursues this study at the university level he will find out, probably too late to make a change, that no matter how good his intelligence, his inborn special ability is equal only to a very moderate success. Similarly, good teaching, much practice, and a keenly emotional desire to succeed may lead to outstanding progress in drawing in the teens. A boy or girl who founds a career on this, without a high degree of special *flair*, is unlikely to scale the heights of even commercial art. It is just in these circumstances that the danger of inspirational teaching lies. Many a boy or girl, through the advice and urging of a beloved teacher, has founded a career on an interest which does not rest on marked innate talents.

Tests of innate aptitudes which are free from the influence of special training and experience are more difficult to devise than tests of intelligence and somewhat less accurate. However, research into their development is proceeding and we have now instruments of measurement which are more accurate than the unaided and merely intuitive judgements even of skilled observers. Tests of mechanical aptitude, consisting of working models which have to be understood by the subject, have been devised by Dr. Cox.[1] A test, the materials of which are the components of a number of common objects, like a bicycle bell or nut, has been used to detect both the comprehension of mechanical principles and the constructive ability to put mechanisms together.[2] Operations involving speed and rhythm of muscular and digital co-ordinations, like putting pegs into holes, aiming at rapidly moving disks, assembling and disconnecting nuts and bolts and so on, have been standardized as measures of manual dexterity.[3] Spatial perception is involved in many tests which use specially shaped blocks of wood as their materials.

[1] *Mechanical Aptitude* (London, 1928).
[2] Stenquist, *Measurements of Mechanical Ability* (Teachers' College, Columbia Univ., New York, 1923).
[3] Pear and Long, *A Classification of Vocational Tests of Dexterity*, I.H.R.B. Pamphlet No. 64, 1932. On the whole subject of Aptitude Testing see Cattell, *Mental Tests* (London, 1936).

Verbal fluency can be tested with material involving speedy word associations, rhyming, and the like. So too drawing, number, and musical ability have all been made the subject of inquiry, and efficient tests have been devised and standardized by means of which comparisons may be made between individuals.[1]

As well as innate aptitude many occupations demand a minimum degree of acquired skill or of attainment in academic subjects. Hence attainment tests are almost equally as important as others. The school record of a child is a valuable guide but it lacks comparative objectivity. A boy who in one school would come top of his form in French or arithmetic, and who would therefore be rated as 'good' in those subjects by his teacher, might in a school where standards were higher only come in the middle or even the bottom of the form, and would in consequence be labelled only 'average' or even 'poor'. The need is thus seen for some comparative measure. This is roughly provided (for some children) by the School Certificate Examination, the passing of which indicates a certain minimum level of attainment. For the child who has not taken such a public

[1] It is of the utmost importance to remember that an *ad hoc* test may or may not measure what it appears to do. The full standardization of a test is a lengthy, complex, and skilled process involving continual experimental choice of materials until a set is found which satisfies two criteria of efficiency as well as possible: (a) that if the test is repeated with the same group after an interval, the results will be closely similar—that is, that the test is *consistent* and *reliable*; and (b) that it measures what it purports to measure with a satisfactorily high degree of efficiency. This is called the *validity* of a test, and is usually gauged by its agreement with some other measure of the quality in question and may be substantiated and refined by the statistical methods of factor analysis. When a test of satisfactory reliability and validity has been built, it is then necessary to establish 'norms of performance'. This is done by administering the test to a large and random sample of the kind of subjects for whom it is to be used. The scores of this group are then arranged in a frequency distribution or curve from which it is possible to tell by how many per cent. of subjects a given score is likely to be exceeded. Individuals can then be graded according to their position relative to the average score or relative to a large and unselected group. Before reliance is placed on any test for educational or vocational guidance, therefore, we should know its precise reliability and validity, and the size and composition of the sample on which it was standardized. On this topic see P. E. Vernon, *The Measurement of Abilities* (London, 1940).

examination, and wherever graduations of attainment have to be measured, there exist standardized tests in such things as English and arithmetic, and most other school subjects.

Interests are more elusive. They can be elicited in the course of an interview and they will display themselves in the field of general knowledge. Of recent years considerable progress has been made, especially by Professor E. K. Strong[1] and his followers, in the construction of what are called 'interest questionnaires' or 'interest blanks', which consist of a large number of topics to which the subject is asked to indicate whether his or her attitude is one of strong liking, indifference, or dislike. Attempts have been made to refine these instruments to the same degree of validity and reliability as has been attained in the intelligence tests; but so far the results, although promising, have not been outstandingly successful. Moreover as we have pointed out previously an expressed interest taken at its face value is not always a reliable guide. Such questionnaires and attitude scales are useful however in indicating extreme cases of individual differences and as a starting-point for planned interviewing.

Closely bound up with the assessment of interests is the assessment of temperament or disposition. There exist a number of tests which purport to measure objectively temperamental characteristics, and in skilled hands these are valuable clinical adjuncts.[2] They fall into a number of types. The most direct are those in which the subject is asked to rate himself or herself on a number of points of character. The difficulty here lies in the fact that few of us are good judges of ourselves, and into any set of answers, all kinds of falsifications, conscious and unconscious, may enter. An attempt has been made to obviate this by the construction of tests which seem to the subject to be measuring something other than temperament or personality. A fami-

[1] E. K. Strong, *The Vocational Interests of Men and Women* (London, 1943).
[2] Vernon, *The Assessment of Psychological Qualities by Verbal Methods*, I.H.R.B. Pamphlet No. 83.

liar example is the June Downey Will Temperament Test,[1] which, using such things as the degree with which the subject can disguise his handwriting, resist suggestion, work under pressure, and the like, attempts to measure underlying traits. Other tests are similar to the Rorschach test,[2] in which the subject is asked to say what ideas are suggested by a number of suggestively shaped inkblots, thus revealing to some extent the contents of his mind. In yet others of these 'projection tests' as they are called, the subject is presented with a picture in which the main character might represent himself and asked to make up a story.[3] Another promising but laborious and cumbersome method is to arrange a series of experimental situations each designed to reveal certain qualities and traits, and then to observe the behaviour of the subject in response to the particular circumstances of each.

All these are subject to at least two disadvantages. Temperament and character are apt to manifest themselves differently in different circumstances and at different times in the life span. The apparently aggressive adolescent, for example, may be compensating for temporary inferiority, and on most other occasions may display a mouselike quietness and circumspection. Those who are acutely conscious of bad traits may be very much on their guard to conceal them and may successfully do so for the brief period of the test. In the study of character and temperament we cannot yet do without 'longitudinal' studies, a record of the development of the boy or girl, man or woman in the formative years of childhood and adolescence. Life history skilfully interpreted will do much to aid our interpretation of present conduct and our prediction of future behaviour, but here again we are up against the lack of objective standards of judgement. Recent research has shown that by breaking down such wide and vague general conceptions as 'character' or

[1] *The Will Temperament and its Testing* (Yonkers on Hudson, 1923).
[2] Rorschach, *Psychodiagnostik* (Berne, 1932).
[3] Raven, *Controlled Projection* (London, 1944).

'personality' into a number of traits, there is a gain in accuracy and objectivity in assessment. If then each trait is carefully defined and graded in three, five, or seven steps to indicate shades from an outstanding to a very low degree of the quality in question, judgement is greatly aided and improved. Finally it is found that two heads or more are better than one, and that if these are trained heads who are agreed upon the interpretation of the trait terms, experienced in assessing personality, and aware of the limitations and fluctuations of their own judgements, they are not likely to be wildly astray in their assessments.

The best method available at present of assessing interest, character, and temperament seems to be a combination of three things:

1. The pooled assessments (preferably gathered over a long period) of a number of judges (such as teachers) made as objective as possible by the use of an analytic scale with whose terms they are quite familiar and in the use of which they have been trained.

2. A number of test situations arranged as informally and as realistically as possible. The ideal would be not to let the subject know he was being tested or observed.

3. An interview with a trained interviewer who understands the techniques and safeguards which should be employed and who can make use either of planned questioning, tests, or anything else at his discretion.[1]

Matching. The art of vocational guidance is, however, more than an intensive study of the child. When all the information has been obtained about a boy or girl, we can construct a kind of diagram, or, as it is called, a 'profile' showing the individual patterning of abilities and qualities. To finish the task of

---

[1] Burt, 'The Assessment of Personality', *B. Journ. Ed. P.* vol. xv, pt. 3, 1945; 'The Reliability of Teachers' Assessments of their Pupils', *B. Journ. Ed. P.*, vol. xv, pt. 2, 1945.

guidance, we need to know at least as much about the occupational field. We need, in fact, to have job profiles built on the
same scheme and expressed in the same terms. Unfortunately
our knowledge here is much less extensive and accurate than
that we can obtain about Jack or Jill with our batteries of tests
and interviews. We know a good deal about broad categories
of occupations; and about certain special jobs and special classes
of job. Many progressive firms have developed their own
personnel departments which conduct research into the best
ways of choosing their employees and matching them with jobs.
Our information at present however is fragmentary and incomplete. The first task of a comprehensive vocational guidance
service, which as we have seen is a dire necessity, will be to push
research systematically forward so that we no longer have to
rely upon rule-of-thumb methods, the vague descriptions in
books on careers, or more or less intuitive judgements.

II. WHAT HAS BEEN DONE?

The incompleteness of our information and the imperfection
of our tools is no excuse for not attempting something more
than mere chance placement of the adolescent in a job. It is
relevant therefore to inquire what means are now in use for
placing adolescents in employment and what plans exist for
expansion and research in this most important field. As long
ago as 1909 special Juvenile Departments were set up at a
number of the Labour Exchanges in England and Wales; and
prior to this, a few Education Authorities had instituted bureaux
to assist boys and girls to choose employment. From then
onwards the service has developed on this dual basis, with 104
out of 315 Local Education Authorities exercising their statutory
powers to maintain Juvenile Employment Bureaux and with the
Ministry of Labour handling the task in other areas, usually
through an office attached to the Employment Exchange. An
essential part of the service has been an *active* committee in

13

each area consisting of representatives of the Education Authority, teachers, employers, workpeople, and others specially interested in the welfare of boys and girls.

The work of this service has largely been limited to fourteen-year-olds leaving what were then called 'elementary' schools. For the grammar-school boy or girl, a number of committees, employment agencies, conferences, Careers' Councils and the like worked before the recent war more or less satisfactorily in various areas. Some schools have appointed 'careers masters' or 'mistresses', and in others the headmaster gives advice; in yet others very little is done.

The Ince Report. In January 1945 a Committee[1] under Sir Godfrey Ince was appointed to report on the Juvenile Employment Service. The report of this Committee points out as a principal weakness of the present system that the service is far from comprehensive. There is no obligation upon juveniles or employers to make use of it, and, in practice, jobs are obtained through heads of schools, private agencies, and the advertisement columns of the press. No figures to show the extent of this are cited in the report but the survey of five Lancashire towns carried out by Professor and Mrs. Jewkes give us a clue.[2] They found that, of 2,000 boys and girls, fewer than one-third obtained jobs through official agencies, a proportion which is confirmed by figures obtained in Merseyside,[3] though the ratio there was slightly higher. Relatives, parents, friends (especially with girls), school, and their own efforts account, apparently, for the most. Some of this failure to use the employment bureau must be traced to a (not always unjustified) distrust of the official; some of it to the forbidding appearance of many bureaux; much of it to lack of publicity for the service and of a clear demonstration to employers, parents and adolescents, of the advantages which it can offer.

[1] *Report of the Committee on the Juvenile Employment Services* (H.M.S.O., 1945).
[2] *The Juvenile Labour Market.*
[3] Caradog Jones, *Social Survey of Merseyside*, vol. iii, p. 212.

The Ince Report insists on the need for a comprehensive scheme which embraces schools of all types, on the need for close co-operation between the school and the employment service, and on the value of disseminating in the schools and among parents, accurate, unbiased, information about careers. The remarkable thing about the document is that it ignores almost entirely (except for the vaguest of references on p. 45) what has been learnt, by experience, of scientific vocational guidance in large experiments carried out between the two wars, going no further in this respect than a previous committee appointed nearly twenty years previously! However, it leaves the way clear for future developments along scientific lines, even if it does little to recognize the methods by which success is most likely to be achieved.[1]

Vocational Guidance Schemes. We may now turn to an examination of the results of Scientific Vocational Guidance. It should be mentioned in passing that most of the work in this country has been carried out either at the National Institute of Industrial Psychology or by investigators loaned by that body to various public authorities. The institute itself has maintained a Vocational Guidance Department since shortly after its foundation in the twenties; and its investigators have carried out schemes on a very large scale in London and in Birmingham. Similar schemes have been, or are, in operation in Edinburgh, Fife, and elsewhere, though the recent war has either caused them to cease or seriously impaired their efficiency. Perhaps the two most remarkable tributes to the practical efficiency of psychological methods of placement are the testing of a million and a half men in the American Army in the 1914-18 war[2] and the comprehensive selection procedures adopted by the British fighting services towards the middle of the 1939-45 war. These have proved so effective in practice that the methods employed,

[1] Rodger, 'The Juvenile Employment Service: Four Comments on the Ince Report', *Occ. Psych*, vol. xx, No. 2, 1946.
[2] Yoakum and Yerkes, *Army Mental Tests* (New York, 1920).

refined by experience, will doubtless become a permanent part of the peace-time organization of the Services.

As a concrete example of a scheme in operation with school leavers over a considerable period we may take the Birmingham Vocational Guidance Scheme.[1] In all, it concerned 1,639 children followed up over a two-year period, and 608 followed up for four years; and has great value since it enables a direct comparison to be made between children who were given the usual guidance of an employment conference held at school (the *Control Group*) and those for whom recommendations were made on the basis of tests, ratings and planned interviews (the *Experimental Group*). The children in the *Experimental Group* were given a series of objective tests—tests of ability to manipulate concrete materials, a group intelligence test, three tests of manual dexterity, two tests of mechanical ability, five short tests of dressmaking ability, and a test of clerical ability. These tests were given by specially trained teachers to the children whilst they were still at school. In addition, the specially trained teachers prepared temperament rating charts, an analysis of the child's personal interests, hobbies, and, as far as possible, social background; and the head teacher of each school supplied a full report on the work and character of each child. In the case of some children, a special home visit was made, and in the case of others, the Medical Officer carried out a special medical examination

When the time of school-leaving approached, the psychologists, the trained teachers, and the Juvenile Employment Officer met in conference, and on the basis of the data enumerated above made specific recommendations for guidance. This advice was later discussed with the parents and child and, subject to the parents' consent, efforts were made to find the child employment along the lines suggested.

[1] Allen and Smith, *The Value of Vocational Tests as Aids to the Choice of Employment*, First Report, 1932; Second Report, 1940. *Scientific Vocational Guidance and its Value to the Choice of Employment Work of a Local Education Authority*, 1944. (All published by the City of Birmingham Education Committee.)

The children in the *Control Group*, received guidance in the normal way. A school report on work and character was supplied by the head teacher; in addition in some cases information from the special medical examination and home visit was also available. The advice given to the child was arrived at in a choice of the employment conference which considered this information; thus the guidance given to the *Control Group* children represented the best that could be done *without* the aid of objective tests and other special procedure. It is important here to remember that this experiment makes a comparison between *two methods* of vocational guidance—the one aided by the instruments of modern psychology, and the other more haphazard; it does *not* draw a comparison between scientific vocational guidance and totally unguided choice; had it done so the results might have been even more striking.

Results. Of the *Experimental Group* 77 per cent. entered posts in accordance with the advice given, whereas only 64 per cent. of the *Control Group* children did so. Of those who entered 'accordance posts' in the *Experimental Group*, 56 per cent. were still in them at the end of two years, and 46 per cent. at the end of four years. In the *Control Group* 37 per cent. only were in the same posts at the end of two years and only 11 per cent. at the end of four. Of the children in the *Experimental Group* who ignored the advice given them, 11 per cent. remained in the same job throughout the four-year period as compared with 26 per cent. of similar children in the *Control Group*. At the end of the follow-up period of two years, 87 per cent. of the posts held by the *Experimental Group* children were in accordance with the advice given, whereas the figure for the *Control Group* is 52 per cent. only. At the end of four years the figures are more striking; 92 per cent. of the children in the *Experimental Group* were in accordance posts, whereas of the *Control Group* only 47 per cent. were.

After four years the children were asked to express their

opinions on the posts which they were holding. Of the *Experimental Group* children in 'accordance' posts 93 per cent. rated them as suitable (60 per cent. as 'very suitable'); of the *Experimental Group* children in 'non-accordance' posts 33 per cent. rated them as 'suitable' (only 19 per cent. as 'very suitable'). Of the *Control Group* children in 'accordance' posts 64 per cent. rated them as suitable (40 per cent. 'very suitable'); and of those in non-accordance posts 78 per cent. rated them as suitable (50 per cent. 'very suitable'). In fact more children in the *Control Group* found themselves satisfied in posts which were *not* in accordance with the advice given them.

The opinions of employers show a similar trend. Of the *Experimental Group* children in accordance posts at the end of four years, only 4 per cent. are rated as unsuitable and 31 per cent. as 'very suitable'. Of *Experimental Group* children in non-accordance posts 15 per cent. are considered 'unsuitable' and 23 per cent. 'very suitable'. Of the *Control Group*, 7 per cent. in accordance and 6 per cent. in non-accordance posts were unsuitable, and 23 per cent. (accordance) and 37 per cent. (non-accordance) 'very suitable'.

We may perhaps summarize this evidence thus. The children to whom advice was given on the basis of tests and special procedure showed a greater tendency to enter posts in accordance with the advice given, to stay longer in them, to find greater satisfaction, and to give better service to their employers than did the children who were advised on the old methods. In addition, tested children in posts not in accordance with the recommendations made do not stay so long, find less satisfaction, are not so highly thought of by their employers, and tend, as time goes on, to enter posts in accordance with the advice originally given. In the *Control Group* the tendency is the opposite. These children pass from posts in accordance with the advice given to posts which are not in accordance with it, and find themselves happier and give better satisfaction to their employers when they are in posts different from the kind they were advised to obtain.

The evidence in favour of the scientific procedures and tests seems to be conclusive. Its general trend confirms the earlier experiments in London[1] and Birmingham; but what is even more important it shows how a large-scale scheme can be carried out in a practical effective way with the minimum disturbance to the schools. Its originators would be the first to admit its imperfections—notably that the information obtained about each child was not matched by an equally objective and comprehensive analysis of the jobs available. Later experiments are attempting to remedy this defect;[2] to use a more elaborate battery of tests and to construct two 'profiles', the one listing the relevant qualities in each child and the degree in which they are present and the other on similar lines for occupations. In that way a more exact matching of the two should be possible. The tests themselves, and in particular the assessments of temperament and of interests, are susceptible of great improvement.

Need for Longitudinal Studies. One thing is however doubly underlined by investigations of this kind. No scheme of vocational guidance which is wedged into the last few months of a child's school career can be more than a partial success. What is needed is a comprehensive programme which combines longitudinal study of the child, from the time he enters school, with appropriate educational and vocational guidance interlocked and articulated at all stages. In a very real sense the allocation of children to different forms of secondary education at 11 +, as is contemplated in the Education Act of 1944, is a disguised vocational selection, since the type of secondary education a boy or girl receives inevitably narrows vocational choice later. The determination, at the earliest possible stage, of aptitudes and interests is thus seen to be one of the most vital

[1] Burt et al., *A Study in Vocational Guidance*, etc.
[2] Macdonald 'A Scheme of Vocational Guidance for Use in an Educational Area', *Occ. Psych.*, vol. xii, No. 4, 1938.

problems confronting the educator; but, as we have seen, with the younger child this is difficult, and, with our present instruments, wellnigh impossible. It is all the more important therefore to insist that the passage from one kind of secondary education to another should be as easy as possible, and that all judgements made of an eleven-year-old child should be considered tentative and subject to revision.

One of the best practical methods of dealing with this is the Multilateral School, such as we discussed in the previous chapter. In the early years of adolescence such a school could provide a common curriculum differentiated to suit different levels of intelligence. Then by continuous guidance the growing youth could be directed into a steadily increasing range of specialized studies as aptitudes and interests declare themselves. Such a realistic conception of education ignores the factitious distinction between cultural and vocational studies while at the same time linking the school as a continuum with the world beyond its gates.[1]

Vocational guidance is one link in the progressive study of the child and the adjustment of education to his needs. Such a scheme of study would include the maintenance of cumulative records, periodic tests carried out by trained teachers, and medical examinations the object of which would be preventive and with a view to later placement in work. Nor should it end with the date of leaving full time schooling. The Ince Report wisely recommends that the Juvenile Employment Bureaux should be closely associated with the County Colleges and at least one of the points of contact between the two should be in the sphere of watching over the child at the beginning of his working life so that the best possible adjustment to work is made. The tapering off of formal education in the later years of

---

[1] Earle, *Methods of Choosing a Career*, and *Tests of Ability for Secondary School Courses* (London, 1936). In these two books, Dr. Earle convincingly argues the case for the multilateral school, the syllabus of which is based upon continued scientific educational guidance.

adolescence must be looked on as a time in which the personality of the youth—his fourfold social, sexual, economic, and spiritual self—has to attain integration and harmony. This will be achieved only through the co-operation of the educator, the vocational adviser, and those in industry whose special responsibility is the welfare of the young employee.

CHAPTER VIII

FULL STATURE

Maturity. Like truth, maturity is difficult to define. In some respects it is an inevitable result of growth and thus a biological concept; but man, more plastic in almost every way than the higher animals, is very much a product of his society and consequently maturity must be thought of also in social terms. And, so little do we know of the intricate relationships of nature and nurture in man that it would be difficult to disentangle completely these two interdependent aspects.

In broad outline, however, the facts of biological maturation are clear. From birth, physical growth continues until the organism attains its maximum height and strength in the late teens or early twenties. Closely parallel to this are a corresponding increase in the absolute power of the intelligence and the emergence of special abilities. Emotionally—though in a less regular fashion—there seems to be development which reaches its peak in the teens with intensifications in such innately determined impulses as those of aggression, gregariousness, and sex, and with a transformation in the total configuration of the emotional life.

These forms of development can be seen as parts of the preparation of the human being for sexual maturity, for mating, and for the protection and nourishment of the young. It is however doubtful whether there exists, or has existed for hundreds of thousands of years, any human society in which the attainment of maturity was no more than a mere biological growth. Man's inveterate tendency to form communities, and the adaptability of his intellectual-emotional apparatus, have led to a steady development of culture and civilization, the survival of which has depended on the passing on, to the new generation, of ideas and ideals held by the old. The more highly developed a society becomes, the wider in scope are those other than biological aims of development and the longer and more difficult is the period of learning and preparation required before the young can be admitted to adult status.

We may admit as fundamental that biological maturity must precede or accompany growth in other directions and take it as axiomatic that the training of youth should foster complete physiological development. Without such a foundation, the maturation of intellect and character will be seriously pre-judiced; but it is little more than a foundation. Without in addition an overriding concept of *social* maturity and some criteria for assessing it, education has little point and, indeed, becomes a mass of unrelated skills.

Intellectual Maturity. The training of the intellect has been accepted as a major objective of education for long enough. Our syllabuses are framed to impart bodies of knowledge and to develop skills and mental habits. Yet maturity of mind is very much more than the possession of an adequate equipment of facts. The man of thirty is probably no more intelligent in a biological sense than he was at sixteen. If he is given tests of reasoning, his performances will show little if any improvement over what he was able to do ten years previously. Yet his mind is probably very different. Increased knowledge in special fields, experience of the likely results of his actions, acquired skills and techniques, the development through use and practice of specific abilities, and the training which he may have received in special directions, should all have combined to make his mind a more effective instrument of his purposes. In this sense, there is no limit to development except that his grasp of the new, whether in ideas or skills, is limited by the level of his innate abilities.

It has been suggested before that intelligence is the moderator, the instrument by which the total needs of the individuality and the demands of the environment are brought into relationship. The effectiveness with which this adjustment is carried out is thus a measure of intellectual maturity. Such a maturity implies, too, something more positive: the development of interests and special capacities to the fullest extent and the bringing of the whole being into the most harmonious and fertile relationship possible with the material and spiritual world.

Emotional Maturity. If intelligence is, as it were, the cutting edge of the mind, emotion is the force behind it. Between the two there is no direct correlation in the sense that high emotionality, for example, is associated with high intelligence or that good intelligence implies, necessarily, adequate emotional adjustment. Not infrequently, in fact, emotional development lags behind intellectual. Nevertheless, as we have already seen, the interrelationships of the two are exceedingly close. Emotional disturbance can inhibit the expression of intellectuality, and the direction of interests as well as their development is dependent upon forces which are instinctive in their origin. In the emotional life, on the other hand, the function of the intelligence is to provide acceptable outlets for the desires which spring from the deepest levels of man's biological inheritance and to interpret the stimuli which arise from the environment. Thus, on the quality of the intellect will depend, in no small measure, the quality of the emotional responsiveness of the individual.

Perhaps the greatest contrast between the developed and mature adult and the young child is in the nature of their emotional responses. The infant is an April day of tears and laughter, no sooner subjected to a stimulus than violently responding to it with some overt action. A sudden noise frightens him to tears which are the next instant dispelled by the diverting of his attention to a bright, jingling bunch of keys. At one moment a little brother or sister may be the object of fierce, possessive affection: the next, of equally demonstrative hatred, or of sullen jealousy. The withdrawal of a toy provokes him to fury, the present of a sweet raises him to the seventh heaven of delight. A similar impulsiveness in an adult would be a sign of marked immaturity. We expect him to look before and after, to be able, in a much greater degree, to inhibit immediate action in response to an emotional stimulus; and we expect his emotional states to be less transitory and less easily deflected.

The ability to inhibit immediate response, and the persistency of the emotional state when once aroused, allow an interval for reflection, and for an adequate choice of response—a choice which should be determined upon intellectual grounds, by the realities of the situation. Hence maturity implies both the inhibition of undesirable and maladaptive desires or expressions of emotion and the ability to find acceptable and serviceable outlets.

Repression and Sublimation. This process of development takes place, principally, through two complementary psychological 'mechanisms', those of *repression* and *sublimation.* The infant, the child, and the youth must learn to curb certain unacceptable forms of behaviour. He must, for example, control those impulses of pugnacity and aggressiveness which would lead him to make a physical attack on anyone who thwarts his will; he must learn that noisy self-assertion is not tolerable; and that over-possessive love or fierce jealousy infringe the rights of others. The impulses which lie behind these and other such desires, however, cannot with safety, be repressed; they are the energies of the mind, and if the attempt is made to suppress them entirely, they will cease to be serviceable to the conscious life and issue indirectly in symptoms of mental or physical illness. 'He who desires and acts not, breeds pestilence'—and that pestilence more often than not is neurosis. The child whose need for affection is not satisfied may compete for attention by sheer naughtiness; the failure to find a legitimate outlet for impulses of self-assertion may result in the boastful liar; a repressed interest in sex which becomes associated with ideas of guilt may issue in an acute and unaccountable anxiety state. Examples from the behaviour of children and adults might be multiplied. The truth which they stress is, not that repression of any kind is wrong, but that repression should be directed at specific undesirable forms of behaviour and not at the impulses which prompt them. Even more important is it that there should be no repression without a corresponding and adequate redirection of energy into desirable channels. It is this redirection of energy which we call sublimation; and general experience shows that those sublimations are the most effective which most closely correspond psychologically with the natural behaviour provoked by the instinctive-emotional disposition concerned.

Conscious and Unconscious Sublimations. The sublimations of the child are rarely made on a conscious level. They depend either upon mere chance or upon the enlightenment of the adults in his surroundings. Opportunities for self-assertion, for example, can be found in constructive activities, in winning the attention and praise of grown-ups for a piece of work well done, in helping, and in learning to do things for oneself. Play, with such aids to fantasy as sand, plasticine, paper and paint, provides another valuable outlet which has been found of value with disturbed children. Greater mental maturity and greater self-knowledge in adolescence and adulthood should mean that sublimations can be sought on a more conscious level, and the adolescent should be helped to find in socially valuable activities —rather than in merely innocuous ones—outlets for the deepest springs of his nature. Aggressiveness and curiosity, for example, may find satisfaction in scientific investigation in which the enemy to be overcome is nature; sex interests may seek direct expression in marriage, collateral outlet in social activities, and a more remote but still serviceable absorption in art, or music, or literature. The woman whose protective and maternal impulses are not satisfied by children of her own may deflect them to caring for the children of others as a teacher or nurse. The desire to dominate and excel may be directed by high capacity into an organizing job or expended in planning a garden or in making furniture as a hobby. Somewhere in the multiplicity of human activities there is to be found one, or a combination of many, which will give free vent to the emotional forces of each youth, and which will satisfy his deepest needs.

The more or less habitual adjustment of the desires to the adult social environment is one mark of maturity. Where, however, the adaptation is *merely* habitual—the result of training rather than of a generalized attitude of mind—a marked change in the psychological environment may cause it to fail. We can see this happening in those cases where the loss of a husband or wife is followed by abnormal grief, nervous breakdown, or even insanity. Some men, satisfactorily adjusted to their civilian lives, developed neurotic symptoms when they were conscripted into the Army. With a few, psychological balance is so precarious that a change of job, or even of workmates, will bring about a crisis.

Adaptability. The enjoyment of mental health and the attainment of emotional maturity therefore imply adaptability, the continuing capacity to find new sublimations when, for some reason, the old ones fail. The achievement of such an attitude of mind is, in great part, dependent upon insight into one's own personality, a knowledge and frank recognition of the needs which demand expression, and on the conscious attempt to find adequate outlets. The intense preoccupation with the self at adolescence, properly directed and enlarged by measuring that self against equals, may be used to foster this self-knowledge, and the maturation of the intellectual power offers a great opportunity for the cultivation of this readiness to seek genuine substitutive satisfactions.

Emotional Freedom. This adaptability implies a balanced expenditure of energy. The truly mature adult will fight no longer than he sees reason, recognizing that there are few disappointments for which no compensation can be found and setting his heart on nothing to the extent that its loss means the loss of everything worth living for. Such an attitude can only be achieved if the mind is freed of what might be called symbolical reactions. The meaning of this is best made clear by examples. The ignorance and suggestibility of the child frequently lead him to emotional reactions out of all proportion to the real nature of the stimulus. The little boy will fly in genuine terror from a growling figure—whom he knows to be his own father masquerading as a bear. A similar but more complex manifestation is seen in the adult obsessional neurotic in whom, for example, a bird or even a feather will arouse a blind, unreasoning fear. Both the child and the neurotic are reacting, not to the objective reality of the circumstances, but to what they symbolize to the mind on a more or less unconscious level. In 'normal' adults, such symbolisms are much more frequent determinants of behaviour than is generally realized.[1] Much prejudice, many irrational aversions, likings and dislikings at first sight, 'intuitive' judgements and the like, may be traced to unconscious complexes and buried memories. It is important that the existence of such disturbing links with the past should be recognized and that they should not be so serious and so powerful as to dominate conscious thinking to any great extent. In this respect, maturity means freedom to see things, events, and people as they truly are and not invested with the unrecognized symbolisms of childhood.

Weaning. Among the most common of these symbolic reactions is that shown by the man or woman who has not truly achieved independence of the parents. If the emotional tie remains powerful, the boy or girl never truly leaves home, even

[1] Freud, *The Psychopathology of Everyday Life* (London, 1914).

if he or she gets married. Marriage, in fact, though perhaps ardently desired, may appear to the unconscious as a threat of loss of parental affection and provoke serious conflict and anxiety, which finds expression in physical or mental breakdown and thus provides the excuse, which is unconsciously desired, for avoiding it. Less extreme cases of dependence result in home-sickness, or a desire to live near the parents after marriage, even though it would be advantageous to go further away. In yet others, the attachment leads to a series of unsuccessful love affairs, all of which fail because the man or the woman is seeking not a mate but a mother or father substitute.

Other symbolic reactions may grow up on the basis of frustrations and repressions. A typical example is the vinegarish spinster who is critical of young and attractive women or who delights in prurient scandal. Deeply repressed antagonisms to parents may find a symbolic object in someone who stands in a similar position of authority—for example a business superior or an employer. Still denied outlet, such aggressions sometimes recoil on the possessor in the form of fears of persecution. Thus we get the picture of the man who believes himself to be the victim of unfair discrimination.

The variety of such developments seems endless. Most of them represent a failure to find adequate outlets for crude and unsocialized tendencies in earlier days, and many are singularly resistant to treatment in any other way than by the revival of the buried conflict from which they arise. The physiological and emotional instability of adolescence frequently provides a mental state in which such buried conflicts become acute. Hence it is not uncommon at this period for serious psychoneurosis, or even some kinds of insanity which rest upon emotional rather than organic bases, to declare themselves decisively for the first time. Schizophrenia, for example, one of the main symptoms of which is an almost total withdrawal from the real world into a fantasy one, is often first diagnosed in the late teens or early

14

twenties.[1] The plasticity of the personality at this time, however, is such that if the early symptoms are tackled in the teens there is some hope of effecting a cure, whereas if the disease declares itself later the outlook is not good.[2]

Methods of mental prophylaxis have already been suggested in earlier chapters. Here it must be reiterated that the plasticity of the emotional life at adolescence and the attainment of full mental growth offer the best opportunity of setting rough places of development right before they have time to become embedded in the adult character. Every means should be taken to provide legitimate and valuable outlets for the instinctive energies. The boy and the girl, at the risk of fostering introspectiveness, should be encouraged to seek self-knowledge and to learn, as far as his or her comprehension extends, the nature of the primitive urges which prompt them and the ways in which they may be satisfied. This means the offering of sublimations and the building up of habits, mental and moral; but it means also the development of independent power to seek satisfaction in many different circumstances, the formation of a general mental set towards adaptability no matter what the demands made by the environment. The revival, in the teens, of buried conflicts from childhood, offers the chance of solving them on a conscious level. The child frequently works out his difficulties in symbolic play; the adolescent can do the same in talk, in drama, in creative work. An impartial adult who can act as the recipient of confidences, a listener who now and then throws in a cheering word; or who, with sympathetic common sense, helps to adjust an exaggerated attitude can, by being himself an objective reference point, bring the youth to a clear mental stocktaking.

[1] Henderson and Gillespie, *A Text Book of Psychiatry*, pp. 289, 328–9.
[2] Gladstern, 'Later Adjustment of Twenty-six Adolescents Diagnosed as Schizophrenic or Potentially Schizophrenic', *Smith College Studies in Social Work*, vol. xii, pt. 2, December 1931.

Maturity of Character.[1] Intellectual and emotional maturity are essential concomitants to maturity of character, which, like the melancholy of Jacques, is compounded of many simples. It must be remembered that intellectual and emotional maturity can be attained within the framework of many different types of character, even within types which in some civilizations would be unacceptable. We must bear in mind too that character is very much a product of the culture within which the individual grows up. Hence our assessment of maturity of character is essentially in terms of what is considered valuable in our own society.

We have suggested already that the adolescent is in search of a self, or rather of an integration of selves, vocational, sexual, social, and moral. It is the sentiments which comprise these which lie at the core of his character; and, dependent upon them, there should be developed a whole series of subsidiary sentiments, some of them abstract ideals of such things as justice, honour, truth, loyalty, and so on, others more specific and concrete, such as give rise to, and maintain, interests in specific directions—in a garden, in games, in a collection of antiques, or stamps; and yet others for particular persons—wife or family, husband, mother, father, children, or friends.

It is from the complexity and relative dominance of such sentiments that there springs the striking difference in quality between the emotional reactions of a child and those of an adult. The child deprived of a beloved toy becomes angry; he looks like anger personified, kicking, stamping, screaming. An adult who is immature may react with a very similar burst of ineffectual fury which would be stigmatized as 'childish'. More likely the response will be complicated; and it will be characteristic, not of adults in general, but of John Jones or Mary Smith in particular; it will be felt to be a part of a whole individual and

[1] What follows in the remainder of this Chapter owes a great deal to McDougall, *Introduction to Social Psychology,* and *The Energies of Men* (London, 1936); and to Aveling, *Personality and Will* (Cambridge, 1931), especially ch. viii.

of a piece with behaviour in other circumstances. Anger at deprivation will probably be felt. It may provide the motive power behind energetic and effective action to regain the lost object. On the other hand, ideals of self-control, preoccupations with other things, a recognition that the cause of the loss is beyond human control, or a willed sympathy with another person's point of view, may lead to a complex variety of feelings and behaviour. One may say that emotional responses in an adult are, as well as being delayed, conditioned and sophisticated by habit and sentiment.

Emotional Responsiveness. Furthermore, the existence of sentiments of a specific or of a general abstract kind heightens emotional responsiveness in certain directions. Events, expressions of opinion, natural objects, and so on may become complex and powerful stimuli to an adult whose sentiments are developed in particular directions, although they would have no meaning whatever to a child. An ancient papyrus to a child may be a dirty piece of paper useless to draw on; to a dealer in antiquities, it may be a valuable piece of stock in trade; to an Egyptologist, a matter of intellectual interest or even something to be defended with his life. There is in the child a certain predictable uniformity and unsophistication in the kinds of stimuli which will provoke emotion. In the developed adult there is some uniformity too, the end of which is to allow the individual to sympathize with and react adequately to the group to which he belongs. Beyond this core of similarity, however, there extends a wide range of individual differences such that a stimulus which would be indifferent to one man, might provoke another to rage, another to protectiveness and another to fear; an object of veneration and love to one may be hatred and derision to another. It is in the broad similarity of fundamental sentiments that we find so called racial characteristics, and it is in the differences between what might be called idiosyncratic sentiments, that we find the differences between individuals of the same race. In the mature adult character we expect to find the development of those sentiments which are necessary to make him an effective member of the group to which he belongs and a compatible development of sentiments peculiar to himself.

Moral Judgement. Even within such a developed system however conflict may arise. Conflict in the child seems to take place on a more instinctive level as a clash between antagonistic impulses. One can often observe a child torn between, for example, fear and desire, between the impulse to take a cake or tart and fear of the consequences of the theft. The ultimate triumph of either impulse depends largely, not upon ideals, nor upon any very remote considerations, but upon the relative immediate strength of the two stimuli. If the cake is very desirable and the chance of punishment remote, temptation will probably prevail. The action of an adult in a similar circumstance may be determined in a number of ways. He may be restrained by fear of the consequences—an essentially childish response. More mature is that in which the temptation is quickly disposed of, or even does not consciously arise, because of an habitual control. Very many of our moral judgements are thus habitual and we are prevented from exhausting conflicts by the cultivation of patterns of reaction adapted to the effortless solution of most of the minor problems of daily life. Some crises, however, arise in the lives of most adults which cannot be dealt with in this habitual way. Then the action taken depends upon the strength and quality of more general dispositions, which reinforce the intellectual perception of what is right. Alone in the face of danger when there can be no question of retribution or even of discovery and when the stimulus to run away is too powerful for merely habitual control, the soldier stands his ground. His perception of the right course is reinforced by an appeal to an abstract sentiment; a powerful ideal of duty, perhaps, or of himself as the kind of person who does not flinch from danger.

It is on the quality of the habitual responses which have been developed and upon the power and content of the sentiments which lie behind them for reinforcement if need be, that much of the value of character depends. Partly, such habits and sentiments are a matter of training in childhood and adolescence; but partly too—especially with the most highly developed characters—they are consciously and deliberately adopted ideals of conduct. In this way, by an intelligently directed will, the individual may grasp higher and higher conceptions and thus maintain and shape his own character.[1]

High ideals and developed habits alone will not ensure consistency. For this there needs to be some master sentiment, an ideal which ramifies and permeates all the others and which is the ultimate arbiter. This integrating sentiment has been identified psychologically as the 'persistence of motives secured by deliberate willing'.[2] As such it has no implication of value and many integrations are possible which would bring effectiveness to the personality. But if we carry the identification of the most desirable master sentiment a stage further and consider it in terms of Western culture, we find that psychologist[3] and poet[4] unite to identify it with the supreme ideal of duty, the Roman virtue of *pietas*.

In the grasping of such an ideal, adolescence is crucial. The attainment of maximum physiological maturity in the intellectual and emotional life, the chance which this presents for re-educating childish attitudes and disentangling unconscious and hampering complexes and the susceptibility to values of adult society brought about by awareness of impending change, make the character more malleable and impressionable than it is ever likely to be again. The years from eleven or twelve to

---

[1] Aveling, *Personality and Will*, p. 168.
[2] E. Webb, *Character and Intelligence*, B. Journ. P. Monograph Suppt., vol. i, No. 3, 1915.
[3] Aveling, op. cit., p. 167.
[4] Wordsworth, 'Ode to Duty'.

eighteen or twenty should be an experimental and a hardening-off period during which it is important to protect the youth from the thwartings, frustrations and cynicisms with which he will be confronted later, and to lay before him worthy goals, habits of thought and ideals which he can take as his own. Step by step, keeping pace with a growing integration of character, the protective control of the adult world should be lessened to the point where it can be finally withdrawn. We must recognize that the highest developments of character are not within the capacity of all and that maturity is a conception balanced between the ideals of society and the handicaps and endowments of the individual. There are some who, through defective intelligence or excessive emotionality, through organic disease or uncontrollable influences in early life, will never adapt, on an adequate level, to our social patterns. The proportion of these is relatively small. The rest, in increasing measure according to their intellectual grasp and the shape of their instinctive-emotional disposition, can be trained in habits of volitional control which shall persist throughout life. They can attain something at least of the calm maturity of the Happy Warrior:

> Whose high endeavours are an inward light
> That makes the path before him always bright:
> Who, with a natural instinct to discern
> What knowledge can perform, is diligent to learn;
> Abides by this resolve, and stops not there,
> But makes his moral being his prime care;
> More skilful in self-knowledge, even more pure,
> As tempted more; more able to endure.
> As more exposed to suffering and distress,
> Thence, also, more alive to tenderness.

INDEX OF SUBJECTS

Adaptability, 191

Adjustment, 16, 28, 34, 41, 60, 94, 191

Adults, 24, 150, 190

Aesthetic education, 67, 140; impulses, 111; interests, 110

Affection, 90

Aggressiveness, 71, 75, 77, 82, 145, 190

Altruism, 114, 116

Anger, 4, 26

Answering back, 1, 71, 77

Anxiety, 5, 23, 34, 36, 42, 81, 82

Apprenticeship, 154

Aptitudes, *see* Special Abilities

Argumentativeness, 30

Art, 103, 122

Atheism, 117

Attitudes, 9, 21, 24, 39, 42, 66, 150

Backwardness, 125 ff.

Behaviour, 1, 14, 21, 27, 31, 40, 45, 71, 87 ff., 95

Biographies, 102, 103

Blind-alley employment, 155

Character, 36, 46, 118, 175, 195–9

Cinema, 44, 107 ff.

Community, 127, 186

Compensation, 35, 160

Complex, 70, 81; Oedipus, 50; Electra, 52

Conflict, 13, 14, 42, 46, 53, 55, 79, 84, 90, 117, 149, 197

Conscience, 39

Contra-suggestibility, 30, 38, 135

Control: loss of, 8; neuro-muscular, 4; self, 64, 196

County colleges, 87, 121, 132, 184

Crush, 42, 59 ff.

Culture, 43

Curiosity, 22, 125, 190

Cyclic insanity, 82

Cynicism, 47, 117, 148, 199

Day continuation school, 121

Day-dreaming, 27, 31 ff., 35, 57, 65, 71, 72, 80, 96, 105, 109, 154, 156, 169

Death, 74, 84–5

Delinquency, 1, 78, 86, 95, 108, 156

Democracy, 133

Diaries, 62, 68, 71, 78, 116

Discipline, 25, 90, 146

Discrepancies of development, 97

Doubt, 116

Dreams, 71, 75, 80, 81

Education, 64, 67, 95, 99, 113, 119, 120, 128 ff.; Acts, 129; co-education, 60, 143; curriculum, 136–41; and democracy, 133; emotional, 66, 127; physical, 104, 140; religious, 142; vocational, 164

Educational backwardness, 125; handicaps, 125; methods, 125, 143, 149; morale, 124, 126; specialization, 141; retardation, 148

Ejaculation, 53

Emotion, 5, 16, 17, 19, 20, 68, 71, 80, 90, 126, 148, 188, 192, 196

Employment, 153; *see* Vocations

Environment, 8 ff., 15, 17, 18, 25, 26, 29, 34, 48

Experimental learning, 112

Family, 1, 14, 25, 39

Fantasies, *see* Day-dreaming

Father and mother, 16, 39, 41, 51, 57, 84

Fatigue, 4, 156

Fear, 4, 23, 24, 26, 33, 34, 74, 77, 81, 82

Fixation, 51

Flirtation, 23, 61

Folie à deux, 85

Food fads, 5

Friction, 25

Friendships, 57, 67
Frustration, 16, 41, 50, 80, 96, 193

Gang age, 2
Gangs, 76, 77
Girls, earlier development of, 3, 7
Glands, 4, 5, 6, 81
Gonads, 6
Gregariousness, 20, 76, 77
Group, 17, 20, 27, 37, 38, 43, 119, 161; methods, 143, 149
Growth, 2, 3
Guilt, 23, 24, 52

Height, 3
Hero-worship, 42, 59 ff.
Heterosexual adjustment, 23, 46; interests, 17, 20, 59
Home, 18, 27, 67, 143; discipline, 25; influence, 29 ff., 161; life, 19, 128
Homosexual experience, 42, 61

Ideals, 38, 44, 113, 115, 118, 198
Identification, 37, 38, 41, 45
Idiots savants, 99
Illiteracy, 107, 120, 124; and emotion, 126
Imitation, 28, 36, 38
Impulses, 87, 189; aesthetic, 111; aggressive, 33, 73, 78, 104, 145; altruistic, 73; egotistic, 79; gregarious, 83, 104; inhibitive, 78, 145; migratory, 83; protective, 73, 77; sex, 79; social, 79
Impulsiveness, 188
Independence, 10, 25, 41, 43, 146
Individual methods, 143, 150; variation, 94, 132
Individuality, 26
Infantile sexuality, 51
Inferiority, 35, 148
Initiation, 9, 10, 24, 119
Injustice, 19, 25
Insecurity, 6, 16, 20, 88
Instability, 47, 88, 193
Instinctive drives: intensification of, 69 ff.; outlets for, 194
Integration, 46, 50, 67

Intelligence, 7, 87, 91 ff., 188; quotient, 92; super-normal, 12, 96; and vocation, 165 ff.
Interests, 22, 58, 67, 83, 160, 174, 195; aesthetic, 110; educational, 121 ff.; increased, 70, 72, 78, 100, 102 ff., 111, 117; vocational, 157
Introspection, 2, 17, 18, 78
Introversion, 169

Job, 153
Joy, 29

Labour market, 159
Labour turnover, 155
Laziness, 97, 148
Learning, 112, 135
Libido, 51
Longitudinal studies, 175, 183
Love affairs, 63
Lying, 79

Maladjustment, 13, 31, 45, 50, 65, 90, 109
Marriage, 9, 10, 14, 16, 41, 46, 50, 63, 153, 162, 193
Master sentiment, 46, 198
Masturbation, 54 ff., 65
Maturation, 92, 154, 186
Maturity, 16, 67, 186 ff., 199; emotional, 188, 195; intellectual, 13, 17, 187, 195; physical, 4, 13; sex, 6, 17; social, 13
Mechanisms, 33, 35, 189
Menstruation, 7, 53, 65
Mentally defective, 95
Metabolic rate, 4, 5
Mid-adolescence, 86
Mimesis, 36
Moods: dejection, 28, 85-6; fluctuations, 15, 71; general, 11, 71-2, 79, 80; happiness, 14 ff.
Moral code, 113; conceptions, 86; judgements, 94, 197

Nature, 19, 102, 103
Negativism, 30
Nemesism, 85
Nervous breakdown, 34
Neurosis, 6, 45, 88, 126, 189, 193

Parents, 1, 14, 16, 19, 39 ff., 47, 56, 66
Personal appearance, 20, 72, 102
Personality, 1, 16, 21, 29, 39, 46; difficulties, 160
Philosophy of life, 59, 67, 86, 101, 113, 119
Physical: activity, 104; change, 2, 3, 5, 6, 8; defect, 35; education, 104; environment, 19; growth, 3, 5, 17; stability, 2
Poetry, 44, 102, 103
Politics, 102, 115
Pre-service units, 128, 147
Primitive societies, 9, 23, 62, 119, 144
Projection, 33, 82
Protective feeling, 77
Psycho-analytic school, 51
Psychological difficulties, 63
Puberty, 5, 6, 7, 9, 23, 24, 49, 53, 99, 144, 145

Rationalization, 34
Reading, 67, 103, 105 ff., 123; excessive, 33
Rebellion, 25
Regression, 31
Religion, 19, 102, 103, 114 ff.
Religious conversions, 87, 114; education, 142; matters, 14; prohibitions, 64; stresses, 11
Repression, 81, 189, 193
Restlessness, 83, 88
Retardation, 100
Running away from home, 84

Schizophrenia, 32, 193
School, 9, 19, 28, 30, 48, 60, 67, 136, 143; leaving, 129; multilateral, 131, 184
Secret societies, 55
Self, 8, 16, 20, 45, 78, 191; assertion, 55, 81, 148, 190; awareness, 26; consciousness, 5, 148, 150; integration, 195
Self-regarding sentiment, 46, 95, 118
Sentiments, 118, 195–8
Sex: adjustments, 52; appetites, 8; behaviour, 21, 56; consciousness, 55; curiosity, 76; development, 48; differences, 7, 22, 72, 105, 144, 145, 163; drive, 23, 49, 82,

116; education, 53, 56, 60, 64, 143; experience, 63; experiment, 14, 44; fantasies, 32; glands, 6; indifference to opposite, 2; maturity, 6, 16; offences, 79; practices, 54, 56; sentiment, 53, 66; stresses, 11; values, 13, 55; wishes, 33
Shyness, 23, 24, 49, 89; emotions, 80
Social activities, 19, 21, 102, 103; pressures, 23
Special abilities, 97 ff., 141, 165; difficulties, 148
Sports, 102, 103
Spurt, 3
Stability, 2, 3
Stress, 6, 9, 11, 16, 23, 29, 34
Sublimation, 13, 80, 83, 95, 116, 189, 194
Suggestibility, 38, 135
Suggestion, 37
Suicidal thoughts, 84
Suicide, 28, 55, 79, 86
Symbolical reactions, 192

Teacher, 7, 12, 16, 24, 42, 47, 142, 148
Teaching, 152, 158
Temperament, 174 ff.
Tests of: attainment, 173; intelligence, 171, 180; mechanical aptitude, 172, 180; special abilities, 171, 180; temperament, 174
Truancy, 96
Types, 45, 99

Unconscious mind, 118
Unemployment, 153, 155
Unhappiness, 18, 19
University, 19

Values, 13, 109, 119
Variation in: behaviour, 87 ff.; development, 193; growth, 3
Venereal disease, 66
Vocational adjustments, 165; ambitions, 87, 141, 163, 178; aptitudes, 165; choices, 14, 157 ff.; guidance, 170 ff.; information, 163; interests, 157; maladjustments, 156; selection, 183

Vocation and: intelligence, 96, 165; personal circumstances, 169; physique, 168; temperament, 168

Wandering, 82 ff.
Weaning, 41, 47, 83, 192

Weight, 3
Withdrawal, 18, 32, 62, 193
Worry, 5

Youth: club, 20, 43, 143; college, 87, 121, 132, 184; leader, 7, 42; movement, 128

INDEX OF NAMES

Ackerson, L., 90
Albert, 84
Alexander, W. P., 98
Allen and Smith, 180
Allport, G. W., 26
Arlitt, A. H., 3, 6, 26
Arnheim, R., 108
Austin, F. M., 159
Aveling, F., 195, 198

Bannister and Ravden, 108
Barnes, L. J., 128
Barnes, 116
Benedict, R., 12
Berdie, F. 160
Binet, A., 92
Blos, H. A., 6, 117
Blumer, H., 110
Blumer and Hausser, 110
Brooks, F. D., 3
Bühler, C., 30, 54
Burgess, 26, 55
Burt, C., 3, 7, 12, 32, 40, 57, 59, 78, 79,
    83, 85, 90, 91, 92, 95, 98, 99,
    100, 101, 108, 120, 124, 126,
    131, 133, 165, 176, 183

Carnivet, N., 55
Carr-Saunders et al., 79, 108
Cattell, R. B., 165, 172
Cole, L. 12, 102
Cox, J. W., 172
Culpin and Smith, 156

Dale, E., 110
Davies, J. G. W., 162
Dearborn and Rothney, 92-4
Dent, E. C., 130
Deutsch, H., 30, 56, 85
Dickenson and Beam, 54
Downey, J., 175
Durant, H., 114

Earle, F., 132, 168, 184

Flügel, J. C., 9, 24, 39, 52, 55, 85
Ford, 108
Freeston, P., 157
Freud, S., 50, 116, 118, 192
Fryer, D. 157
Furfey, 2

Gesell, A., 12
Gladstern, H., 194
Gordon, H., 95
Gray and Munroe, 105
Green, J. A., 106

Hadow Report, 130
Hall, S., 1, 9, 11, 54, 86, 115
Hamilton, G. V., 62, 63
Hardy, 108
Hart, B., 32
Harvard Committee, 136
Havelock Ellis, 52, 54
Hazlitt, V., 91
Healey, W., 91
Henderson and Gillespie, 6, 194
Hollingworth, L., 7, 11, 30, 55, 63, 115
Holzinger, K. J., 98
Howard, B. A., 144
Howe, G., 84
Hurlock and Jansing, 162

Ince Report, 178, 179, 184
Iovetz Tereshchenko, 58, 62

James and Moore, 154
Jenkinson, A. J., 105, 108
Jewkes, J. and S., 168, 178
Jones, Caradog, 155, 178
Jones, E., 52, 55, 117
Jones and Hsai, 92
Jordan, A. M., 105-6
Jung, C. G., 114

Kaplan, 164
Kenworthy, 154
Kimmins, C.W., 75
King, 126
Kitchen, P. I., 128, 147
Knight, R., 92
Kuhlen and Lee, 61

Lancaster, W., 103
Lane, Fearnley, 87
Lehmann and Witty, 157
Lummis, P., 96
Lush, A. J., 153

Macaulay and Watkins, 86
Macdonald, 183
Mannin, E., 52, 55
McCurdy, J. T., 56, 81
McDougall, W., 36, 50, 117, 195
Mead, M., 13
Mercer, E. O., 163
Meredith, G., 62
Miller, E., 50, 108
Miller, H. Crichton, 50, 52
Moll, 52
Morgan, A. E., 106, 108
Morton, F., 144

Norwood East, 90
Norwood Report, 130
Nunn, T. P., 36

Pallister, M., 159
Partridge, 12, 64
Paul, Eden and Cedar, 56
Payne Fund, 109
Pear and Long, 172
Phillips, M., 111, 141
Pilgrim Trust, 153
Pratt, 116
Prideaux and McDougall, 50

Raphael, W., 155
Raven, J., 175
Read, C. S., 54, 55
Report: Curriculum Reform, 136;
    Hadow, 130; Ince, 178, 179,
    184; Norwood, 90; Spens, 130

Richardson and Stokes, 92
Rodger, A., 156, 170, 179
Roeber and Garfield, 160
Rorschach, H., 175
Rothney, P. 104

Schonell, F. J., 126
Shakespeare, J. J., 99
Simmonds, P., 3
Simson, W., 22
Smith, M., 156
Smith, Culpin and Farmer, 156
Spearman, C., 91
Spencer, F. H., 108
Spens, 130
Starbuck, E. D., 87, 116
Stenquist, 172
Stott, M. B., 163
Stout and Mace, 36
Strong, E. K., 174
Symonds, P., 15

Terman, L. M., 7, 12, 64, 94
Terman and Lima, 105, 106
Thouless, R., 36, 49, 116
Thurstone, L. L., 98
Trotter, W., 11

Valentine, C. W., 26, 28, 37, 52, 57,
    61, 84, 85, 101, 103, 144, 158,
    159
Valentine and Emmett, 96
Varendonck, J., 31
Vernon, M. D., 161
Vernon, P. E., 38, 99, 173, 174
Viteles, M., 7

Wall, W., 95, 120, 124, 126
Watts, A. F., 101
Webb, E., 198
Wheeler, O., 59, 61, 79, 101, 103, 117
Williams, H. D., 32
Williams, T., 90
Winsloe, Christa, 42
Wray and Ferguson, 124

Yates, 64
Yoakum and Yerkes, 179

For Product Safety Concerns and Information please contact our EU
representative GPSR@taylorandfrancis.com
Taylor & Francis Verlag GmbH, Kaufingerstraße 24, 80331 München, Germany

www.ingramcontent.com/pod-product-compliance
Lightning Source LLC
Chambersburg PA
CBHW050436280326
41932CB00013BA/2141